PRAISE

Beyond 1%: Unleashing Your Potential Against All Odds

"Brock Mealer's journey from tragedy to triumph is a testament to the power of perseverance and resilience. His story reminds us that no matter the obstacles we face, with determination and faith, anything is possible."

—Brandon Graham,
Philadelphia Eagles Defensive end and Super Bowl Champion

"Brock Mealer's story is a must-read. I got to witness firsthand his amazing determination, faith, and dedication to overcoming the odds! His positivity in the face of tremendous adversity was truly inspiring to myself and our entire program. Whether you feel like things are tough and not going well or you just want to read about a true success story, this book will motivate you to keep working hard!"

—Rich Rodriguez,
Head Football Coach at Jacksonville State University

"Sometimes we're tested not to show our weaknesses, but to discover our strengths. Brock has exemplified this and has become a beacon of hope and inspiration to us all."

—Lomas Brown,
Former Detroit Lion Football Player and Current WJR Broadcaster

"Buckle up your chinstrap, and get ready for Brock to take you on a journey so moving that it will forever change your perspective on what is humanly possible. Not only did he find the strength and courage to survive and rise above his own tragedy, but he has dedicated his life to seeking out others during their darkest hour to give them the one medicine their doctors were not able to prescribe—HOPE! Brock's true story will lift you up when you are feeling down and recharge your soul. He reminds us all that no one should ever tell you what you are capable of. Only YOU can set that limit!"

—Thomas Orr,
Clearwater Marine Aquarium, Past Chairman

"Brock's response to the tragic events that happened to him is a real-life example of how to turn tragedy into triumph. As evidenced by his faith and hard work, *Beyond 1%: Unleashing Your Potential Against All Odds* is a testament to the willpower of the human spirit."

—Parker Whiteman,
Head Strength & Conditioning Coach, Jacksonville State University

"Reading Brock's courageous story will instill in you, as it did in me, the belief that you can accomplish your goals if you believe anything is possible and that you have unwavering faith to help guide you through your journey."

—Tim Dougherty,
VP of Sales, Ariat Int.

BEYOND 1%

UNLEASHING YOUR POTENTIAL AGAINST ALL ODDS

BROCK MEALER

Published by Storybuilders Press

Paperback 978-1-954521-36-0
Hardcover 978-1-954521-37-7
eBook 978-1-954521-38-4

To my family: Mom, Blake and Molly, and Elliott.
You lifted me up when I was at my lowest.

In loving memory of my dad, David Mealer, and
Hollis Richer, who continue to inspire us every day.

CONTENTS

FOREWORD

I believe that sometimes God takes advantage of the adversity we face to mold us into who we're supposed to be. When you're in the middle of a storm, and you can't see the sunshine as the rain crashes down on your face, all you need is for the clouds to part just enough for you to look up and see just one ray of sunshine to give you a little bit of hope.

Sometimes it feels like the clouds may never part, and that's when *you* have to become the ray. And if you can get to a point where you can be that ray, inspire somebody to run through the storm and come out on the other side—it will change your life.

I was working with my wife, Autumn, running the Sports Science Division at West Virginia University during their Golden Era in sports. We were one of the winningest programs in the country at the time. We had a lot of blue-collar, tough kids who just kind of ground it out and turned themselves into highly successful athletes through the training regimen we built and the hard work they put into it.

The university's athletic programs were successful, which meant the kids themselves were succeeding, but I still felt like I could do more. I talked to Autumn about how even though we were at the top of our game, I didn't feel like I was personally doing all that I could do with my physiology background.

I remember Autumn telling me, "You already work seventeen hours a day. Every other school wants what we're doing with this program. If you feel like there's something else to do, you better start praying, because it's obvious that you can't just show up and do more work."

In 2007, at the absolute pinnacle of their success, West Virginia's football team suffered a heartbreaking late-season loss to Pitt, killing their dreams of a national championship. Instead of meeting with head coach Rich Rodriguez and the other coaches after the game, I went home, intending to be with my family and think about how I could help the student-athletes learn from this loss heading into our postseason, non-championship bowl game.

When I went into my office early the next morning, the coaches were all gathered there. They had met with Rich the night before, and he told them he had been in talks with the University of Michigan over the last several weeks, and because of some issues happening with the higher-ups at WVU, he wanted to make a move to the Wolverines. And he told them he didn't want to go without me.

It didn't take me long to realize the possibility that this situation was God answering my prayer to make better use of His gifts to me by opening a new door of opportunity. Long story short, I made the move to the University of Michigan with Rich after finishing my commitment to the WVU team that season. An almost unbelievable chain of events was put into motion.

The first two players I met when I walked into the facility at Michigan were Brandon Graham and Elliott Mealer. I joked around with Brandon for a little bit and then turned my attention to Elliott.

His arm was in a sling after a recent rotator cuff surgery. We talked about how he had convinced his dad, an unwavering Ohio State fan, to let him visit Michigan, "that place up North" and home to OSU's biggest rival. Elliott talked about how he felt like God called him there, and that after the visit, and with his dad's blessing, he accepted their offer to play for the Wolverines.

Both of us were there, at that moment, because we believed God had brought us there. And I don't believe it was a coincidence.

Elliott asked me if I'd mind going to see his brother in the hospital. I asked him what had happened. After hearing the story Elliott shared, I immediately agreed to go with him. It was supposed to be my first day of coaching, yet I skipped the coaches' meeting and went to the hospital instead.

When I met Brock that day, I could not believe his positivity. He was in really bad shape, but he was smiling and thanked me for visiting.

That meeting was the beginning of the craziest journey of my life. Brock was the catalyst that God, through Elliott, had put in front of me to help me find my greater purpose in life. I am honored to be a part of Brock's life. I love him, and I love his family.

I'm just the guy who got to be there to see what God can do when you embrace the struggle and put your faith in

Him. What happened to Brock and his family was a horrible tragedy, but the positive ripple effect that their experience started is immeasurable. It's my honor to introduce you to Brock Mealer and his inspiring story.

Mike Barwis

Founder and CEO of the BARWIS Family
of Companies, Including BARWIS
Methods Training and ARS Screening, BARWIS Neurological
Reengineering, BARWIS Performance Centers and Equipment
Director of Sports Science Detroit Red Wings
Director of Sports Science Anaheim Ducks
Former Consultant Miami Dolphins
Former Director of Sports Science University of Michigan
Former Director of Sports Science West Virginia University

INTRODUCTION

A first step toward something new can be described with many different words: *bold*, *decisive*, *frightening*, *courageous*, *exciting*, or even *definitive*. It can also be described as *successful* or *failing*, which can bring up many different emotions in people.

When I think of taking an initial stride toward something, I remember so many times in my life when I took a chance to start something new. But I certainly can't remember walking for the very first time as a toddler.

I wonder what words I would have used to describe it, or the emotions I might have felt about doing something so new to me. I also wonder what emotions go through a parent's mind while their child is finally starting to walk. It is such a milestone in our lives and is remembered as a great accomplishment.

What no one remembers is how many times a toddler falls before they can stand and walk. Or how many times that child falls over the years as they grow up. Falling is a normal part of life. And so is getting back up.

Sometimes getting back up feels like the most difficult thing you'll ever do. There is some truth to the idea that the first step is often the hardest. It's moving away from where you are and into the unknown. But it's also a testament to your faith, commitment, and capacity for growth. I've had my fair share of facing uncertainty in my life. But even when it felt like I had nothing left, I still had hope.

CHAPTER I

LOSING CONTROL

In September of 2007, my girlfriend left for Nice, France, to study abroad as part of her college experience. I tried to push away my fear that our almost four-year relationship could change over the span of the three short months that she would be there. We planned to meet in Paris for a mini vacation a few days before she was scheduled to return to the States and then fly home together.

When I surprised her by coming to visit her in Nice at the halfway point of her trip, it didn't feel like the romantic gesture I thought I'd created for us. I met some of her new friends and came home feeling uneasy about our relationship. But I flew home with all her reassurances that we were okay, so I let the busyness of working part-time at our family's concrete business lift my spirits with a renewed sense of purpose.

The closer the days got to our Paris trip, the more nervous I began to feel. We were talking on the phone weekly, for the most part without consequence. But two weeks before I was supposed to depart, I felt the need for a check-in with her. I told her I planned to have dinner and an important conversation with her parents, but I could hold off if she wanted me to. She picked up on my hint. She definitely wanted me to meet with them and said she had no doubts about our future. With her response in mind, I called her parents and then made our reservation.

We met at an Italian restaurant outside of Toledo, Ohio, and despite all our previous get-togethers, they knew this dinner was unique. I had picked up the ring that morning, and when I told them about my proposal plans, they seemed more reassured than surprised. I couldn't help but share some of my concerns about our relationship without going too deep into the details, and they both confidently affirmed that there was nothing that would make their daughter change her mind. I agreed, but I reiterated that I just wanted them to be aware that it might not go as we planned. They continued to build me up and boost my confidence, which helped but didn't completely erase my fears.

As the days rolled on, I felt more at ease about the trip and the proposal. I started visualizing our future together while trying to keep some level of focus at work that Friday, just one day before my planned departure. And then I received a surprise instant message from her on my lunch break. After some hellos, she jumped right in and asked how I'd feel if she didn't meet me in Paris.

My heart sank.

She went on to say that she just couldn't leave her new friends for three days. She knew what was at stake and said she was sorry, but that was just how it had to be. When she said she had to go, the reality of the situation made my future seem more clouded and darker than I could have imagined.

Feeling sick, I headed home. There was a deep pain in my chest as tears poured down my face. I sat on my bed with my face in my hands, praying to God and trying to wrap my head around what had just happened.

How is this even possible? Why would this happen to me? What did I do that was so wrong?

I simply could not comprehend such a bitter and flippant rejection from this person who was such a huge part of my life.

What was I going to do about the trip? What would I say to my parents—and to hers? How could I explain something that made no sense to me?

FINDING STRENGTH IN SURRENDER

At a moment when I felt like I had a clear vision for my future, something I had no control over completely turned my world upside down. There was no avoiding the fact that my relationship was over, and I remember thinking there was no way to fix the part of my life where I'd invested so much.

My dad let me know it didn't matter if I couldn't get the money back for my ticket. He said I should just be home with the people I loved and let it go. I knew he might be right, but I couldn't help but wonder whether it might be healing for me to make a solo trip of the one I had initially planned for someone else to experience with me.

At this point, I was supposed to leave within hours. After agonizing over what to do well into the night, I finally made the decision: I was going to Paris. It wasn't an easy choice by any stretch of the imagination, but I knew it was a trip I had to take. I embraced it as an opportunity to grow and discover more about myself. I wanted to make the most of it, even though I had no idea what would come of it, if anything.

On the flight, I had time to process all the emotions I'd experienced in the span of a week. My now *ex*-girlfriend's mom had given me a journal, and I just started writing whatever popped up, grateful to have a place to gather my thoughts. I was also thankful for her husband and the kind words he always had for me. I appreciated their compassion when I explained that the relationship was over and I wouldn't be proposing after all.

My older brother-Blake, my dad-David, myself, my mom-Shelly, and younger brother-Elliott

I was even more grateful for my family. My brothers were always there to help me keep going forward. My mom gave me the will to be strong. And then there was my dad, the one person I could always confide in. His words of wisdom, love, and incredible sense of humor have helped me countless times throughout my life, but most especially in that moment.

Most of all, I thanked God, my Lord, Savior, and Redeemer. I believed that He already knew I would overcome my situation. I started to feel like maybe I had become complacent in my faith. I began to feel as though God wanted to have me closer to Him, praying and going to church more regularly. The more I prayed and leaned into my faith, the more I began to understand that God wanted to be with me, to feel what I felt, and to become a necessary part of my life.

As I battled with thoughts of sadness, frustration, and thankfulness, I asked myself a question: *With all the good things in my life, how could I complain about this one thing that was taken from me?*

I believed God would bless me if I put Him first. I didn't know *how* He would bless me on that trip, but I did know it was another opportunity to grow. I had to surrender to His will and go with the flow, even though my heart felt numb.

When I talk about surrendering, it actually has nothing to do with giving up, throwing in the towel, or waving a white flag in the air. For me, surrendering meant prayerfully considering my next move and having the faith that God was right beside me, helping me move forward. With that relationship, I saw the red flags popping up, but I wanted things to work out the way I had envisioned our future together. I wanted to control the narrative so badly that I kept pressing forward despite those nagging feelings that it wasn't going to work.

There's a certain amount of comfort we feel when it seems like we're in control of our own outcomes. But when we lose that control, it can leave us falling into a downward spiral. In our darkest moments, the only things we may be able to see are pain and despair. But in those moments, we also have the choice to let go and let God take over.

CHRISTMAS EVE

A month or so later, on Christmas Eve, a single moment in time redefined *surrender* for me exponentially. I was just a week away from starting my last quarter of college at The Ohio State University, beginning to look forward to leaving 2007 behind and letting the new opportunities ahead of me begin to unfold. I never imagined that in less than twenty-four hours, my entire life would become unrecognizable.

I think I surprised my dad when he greeted me from the kitchen that morning, telling him I was going out for a run in the wintery Ohio weather. As I shut the door behind me and took in the snow-covered yards and wet concrete, I wondered if I should just join my dad for breakfast and run when the weather was more cooperative. I remember shaking off the random thought, *What if this was my last opportunity to run?*

Braving the elements, running a few miles toward an insignificant location as the snow melted on my face, I decided to enjoy every moment—every near slip in the snow, every hard-fought breath of cold air, and the chance to forget about losing the love of my life in a breakup of epic proportions.

As I finished my run, I could still feel the burn of the cold on my face. My legs and hands were cold and damp from the snow melting as it landed on my skin. I remember feeling an incredible sense of accomplishment for such a short run. The relatively enormous challenges I had recently overcome gave me a renewed sense of strength and encouragement in knowing the worst was finally over. I felt fortunate and appreciative of all the things I had in my life and was optimistic about the future again.

These feelings were reinforced as I entered the house and was welcomed by my dad finishing making breakfast. The smell of bacon and eggs filled the room. I was ready to eat a warm meal after the exhilaration of running through the cold, wintery weather.

There were few things I enjoyed in life as much as the time I had talking one-on-one with my dad. He always had a way of knowing how I was feeling without having to ask, but he often *would* ask, almost as if he just wanted to let me know he cared. Growing up, he always had a way of being stern but making sure I understood why. He also made sure I knew that what we took for discipline wasn't his favorite thing for us, but it was necessary. It definitely was something that gave each of my siblings and me self-discipline.

Having cleaned up after my run and eaten my late breakfast, I went back upstairs to my room and played my guitar. It was the way I had spent much of my free time, trying mainly to learn The Beatles songs—my dad's favorite band that became my own. I remember him telling me that when his father (my grandpa) passed away, he would listen to The Beatles in his room to escape from reality. My dad was still in high school at that time. I never knew his dad, but I often heard stories about him.

As I continued my own escape from reality in my room, I began wrapping gifts. My older brother, Blake, was with his in-laws in Indiana, so I set his gift aside for the next time we got together. I always enjoyed taking the time to find a gift that was particularly special to the person I was giving it to, which took time. I wasn't able to do it every year, but this particular Christmas, the unique circumstances led me to focus on my family. I found respite by focusing on the people in my life who still cared about me.

Our family gathered in the living room and kitchen as we prepared to leave for the annual Christmas party at my mom's cousin's house, about thirty minutes away. My brother Elliott's girlfriend, Hollis, had just arrived. As she came into the house, Elliott greeted her with a gift. She was happy, as always, to see everyone, but even more so that Elliott had a surprise for her. She opened the package to find two rings he simply couldn't wait any longer for her to have.

THE MOMENT OF IMPACT

There was a light snow falling outside, just enough to see it on the concrete driveway. As we approached our silver Mercedes SUV, I walked toward the door behind the driver's seat. My dad reached for my shoulder and told me I should ride shotgun, next to him. I obliged, although my mom usually sat up front when we were on family excursions. I could tell this occasion was different simply because of the extra-special treatment my dad had given to me during the last couple of weeks of heartache.

As we arrived at the party, we were greeted by my grandma's siblings and the smells of all our traditional Christmas Eve food. Every year, their garage was transformed into a giant dining room with people coming and going between visiting with one another and playing pool and other games in the basement.

Around nine o'clock, we started to feel the party winding down. As our group began to think about gathering our things and saying our goodbyes, my mom told me that Hollis was feeling under the weather. We were in the kitchen, but I could see Elliott in the hallway, just outside of the bathroom with a look of concern on his face. She tried to minimize how she felt, but we let her know it wouldn't be a big deal and we were ready to go anyway. My grandma tried to get one last photo of us before we left, but we decided we didn't want to make Hollis feel uncomfortable any longer than necessary.

My mom sat behind my dad on the driver's side, while Elliott squeezed into the middle to let Hollis have the window seat behind me. I settled into my seat, resting my arm on the armrest and holding on to the door handle as I leaned my head back to rest my eyes.

We kept the conversation to a minimum, mostly to give Hollis some peace and quiet. When we were a few miles from home, I looked off into the distance and noticed the blotched whiteness of the snow across the fields. I casually turned to my left to look at a house on the corner of the intersection. That's when I saw a small car speeding toward the stop sign. My mom shouted for my dad to watch the car, and almost immediately, I felt the impact as it hit our driver's side rear tire.

My stomach sank as our SUV's rear end started to shift. My eyes turned along with the motion to the left as I screamed. The SUV had just started to roll as it completed a one-eighty, and I blacked out.

A WAKING NIGHTMARE

As I came to, I was lying on my right shoulder. I looked to my left (which was up, from my angle) to see the driver's seat empty. I immediately looked to the back seat and saw it was empty as well. I couldn't comprehend what was happening, but I felt a brief moment of relief that everyone else was out of the car.

The radio was still on and playing "It's Beginning to Look a Lot Like Christmas." Crying, I hit the Power button, but the music continued. I began punching the audio screen I had put in just a few years ago, desperately wanting to stop the music. I didn't know if stopping the music would help me think or if I was just angry, in disbelief of what had happened. It finally stopped.

I reached for my cell phone and called 911, not knowing whether anyone else had done so yet. Had they just climbed out of the car? How long had it been since the accident happened? The 911 operator asked what the situation was. I told her someone ran a stop sign near a local restaurant, just outside our hometown. Our vehicle was on its side, and I couldn't see or hear anyone else. She told me that help was on the way and to stay calm. The call ended, and I threw my phone to the floor.

All I knew was that I wanted to get out of the car. It seemed it was all I *could* do, after shouting for help and waiting for anyone to respond. I began to press the floor with my legs and reach for the sunroof just above and in front of me so I could start climbing to the driver's side window. I barely moved. I squeezed each of my legs with my left hand; I couldn't feel my hand squeezing my thighs. I couldn't feel anything in my legs, and I couldn't understand what was going on, but I moved to see if my seat belt was holding me down. I hit the button with my left hand, then tried to reach up with both hands.

I suddenly realized my right arm was trapped. My wrist was pinched in the few inches of space between the long door handle that ran vertically and the door itself. I repeatedly tried to rip my arm from the handle's grasp and failed. I knew if I could just free that hand, somehow my legs would work and I could get out. My wrist looked like it was made of rubber as I pulled and stretched it, but the pain was excruciating.

Knowing I needed help to get freed, I stared blankly into the shattered glass that used to be the windshield. I thought I heard some shouting in the distance, so I turned my head as far to the left as I could to try and see out the rear window. The glass was gone, and I saw an elderly man with glasses and a long white beard wandering around. I thought I must be in the middle of a nightmare and I'd wake up soon once I realized I'd dozed off on the way home from the party. I could see the thickness of the man's glasses when he turned, barely able to walk. I wondered if he was hurt, and then I wondered why his glance passed by me as if the car wasn't even there. I later learned that he was the ninety-two-year-old man who ran the stop sign.

Terror set in as my mind began to come back to me from the daze I'd been in. I didn't know how much time had passed since I made the 911 call, but I started to see some flickering lights and noises outside.

Suddenly, a black shadow approached, and I wondered if it was the Angel of Death. Instead of scaring me, it brought me a comforting feeling that maybe the nightmare was coming to an end. I remembered praying to God to send an angel at some point, but I couldn't foresee what God had planned for me.

The shadow was actually an EMT who was there to help. He asked if I was in any pain, and I responded that my right arm was trapped and was as numb as my legs. When he asked if the man beside me was breathing, a new wave of shock and confusion rushed through me. When I turned toward the ground, I saw the back of my dad's faded leather jacket. The tears once again streamed down my face when I put my left hand on his back and couldn't feel him breathing.

Suddenly, I no longer cared about getting myself out; I knew my dad needed to get out. I couldn't comprehend how he had been there that whole time without me realizing it. There simply wasn't room for my dad to be there, but somehow he was. I continued to cry and punch the dashboard as I waited.

When the man returned, he gave me a blanket to cover myself so glass and debris wouldn't cause more damage when they used the Jaws of Life. I covered up and closed my eyes. The hydraulic sounds of the machine seemed to be right in front of me as I heard crunches, crackles, and thuds. Fragments of the SUV flew into my arms and then all the noise was replaced by voices.

People were pulling the windshield off. I could see a bright light through the back of my eyelids. The same voice let me know I could take the blanket off. He was kneeling in front of me. They were able to get my dad out, but I didn't realize it. I didn't even know if I was still sitting in my seat anymore. The voice told me they were going to get my arm out first.

Two men grabbed a part of my shoulder and arm, counting down as they prepared to pull. I glanced over to see as my hand stayed in the door handle while the men tugged on my arm and shoulder further and further. They slowly pulled ... one, two, and then three ... I was free, but my right hand seemed to hang off the bottom of my arm.

The first EMT I saw came back again, kneeling down at eye level. He stared me straight in the eye through his glasses.

"We're going to get you out onto the stretcher and get you to the hospital. Just to be clear with you, this is going to be extremely painful, and I don't want you to be shocked."

I nodded but didn't understand. I know I had told him how my arm was numb, just like my legs. I felt some soreness, but nothing that seemed all that painful to me.

"I just want to get out of this car, whatever it takes," I told him with confidence, or maybe ignorance.

Two men stood at each shoulder. The man talking grabbed my feet to lift, counted to three, and I felt the most unbearable pain I'd felt in my life—as if someone had hooked battery cables to each foot and a surge of electricity was running through my entire body. I screamed out in pain as they laid me flat onto the stretcher. What had to be the last of my tears pressed out of my eyes, and I couldn't breathe as they strapped me down. The initial shock was over, but the pain seemed to continue to pulse through my body.

I was placed into the ambulance and driven to the Fulton County Health Center, just inside my hometown of Wauseon, Ohio. They wheeled me into the emergency room as a doctor or nurse told me they would have to cut off my leather jacket and shirt. I told them it didn't matter to me, to do whatever they had to do.

I seemed to enter a state of apathy, as my emotions were drained, and I felt as if nothing mattered to me. I still wanted to believe it was all a horrible nightmare, but the intense pain made it too real to reject reality. I didn't know whether accepting it as reality would help or if letting myself feel completely numb would get me through. The nurses pushed me into an X-ray machine and then sent me into another room to wait.

My older brother, Blake, was there as soon as I arrived. He was crying as he grabbed my hand, and I couldn't help but cry again. As he was telling me I'd be okay, and that we would get through this, a state trooper in full uniform came into the room. I thought he might be there to ask about what happened, but I had no idea. He looked at my brother and me with the straightest of faces and told us how much he regretted informing us that our father had passed.

Suddenly, my eyes found an abundance of tears that I thought had been completely used up. I completely lost control of my emotions. Any thought of whether this was reality or a nightmare went out the window. There was only this moment.

A nurse reluctantly interrupted our devastation to inform me that I needed to be taken to a bigger, better-equipped trauma hospital in nearby Toledo, Ohio, immediately, and I had to leave my family behind. I was alone in unimaginable pain and grief.

After a torturous second ambulance trip, I arrived at St. Vincent's Hospital in Toledo. Someone told me I was going into surgery immediately. She asked me to start counting down from ten as she placed a mask on my mouth."Ten, nine, eight ... "

Then everything went black again.

LIFE IS UNPREDICTABLE

I can honestly say that I thought I'd hit rock bottom when my girlfriend broke up with me in an instant message. I could have never predicted what was going to happen on that ride home from the Christmas party a month later. I wanted to begin this book by sharing this part of my story with you, not to make you feel sorry for me, but to set the stage by showing you how this horrible accident wasn't the end of my life's story but rather the beginning of a different one I could never have predicted.

Wherever you are right now, even if it's your own version of rock bottom, it isn't the end of your story either. I'm here to tell you that through any and all unforeseen circumstances, we always have one thing we can control—how we choose to respond.

On the pages to come, you'll have the opportunity to recognize and take ownership of your own circumstances as you lean in and learn more about yourself, and then find a way to use your God-given gifts to achieve more than you ever imagined possible.

Think about standing at the bottom of a mountain looking up. Something deep inside you knows there is an incredible opportunity waiting for you at the peak, but no matter how hard you squint or adjust your binoculars to see it, there are clouds blocking your view. Instead of giving in to any feelings of overwhelm or discouragement, or worrying about potential obstacles in your way, both seen and unseen, just gather your strength and take one step forward.

That one tiny act of faith may seem insignificant, but as you keep pushing forward, there will come a time when you look back and see that the first step you took in faith led to so much more than you could ever imagine for yourself. After my accident, I came to understand just how life-changing that one small step can be—literally.

CHAPTER 2

NEGATIVE AND POSITIVE

I had a much more peaceful awakening after my first surgery at some point on Christmas Day, but I still had no concept of time. I felt like I had just finished my countdown from ten to zero and woke up by accident. A doctor and two assistants walked up to the end of my bed shortly after I was awake and a little more aware.

"Your surgery lasted over eight hours, but we were able to complete it successfully. It took longer due to the numerous and tiny fragments of vertebrae that were shattered in your back. Your T12 and L1 vertebrae were completely replaced, and they'll become stable with time."

"Unfortunately," she proceeded, "you have suffered a spinal cord injury during the accident, which is untreatable. We fully expect that you will never walk again. If we had to take a shot in the dark at your chances of walking, let alone feeling or moving your legs, it would be optimistically placed at one percent. I've performed over a thousand surgeries, and based on the trauma to the bones surrounding the spinal cord, you'll be fortunate if our tests show that it isn't a complete injury with the spinal cord completely severed."

Suddenly, my future seemed as dark as the times when I had blacked out. The surgeon went on to explain some of the recent innovations in spinal cord injuries and the potential for a cure in the future, but there wasn't much they could do about my recovery until they controlled my complications and the swelling went down. She continued by asking if I had any questions, and the only one I could think of was whether or not I would still be able to have kids.

She had a slight smile on her face as she told me I would be able to. That at least gave me something bright to hope for in the future—that, and a one-percent chance of changing how traumatic and tragic this situation was.

With everything that had happened that I couldn't change, I felt like this seemingly impossible task was the only thing with the slightest chance to change. Just when hope already seemed to be at its lowest, it managed to dwindle even further.

Thankfully, several days later when test results came back, we found out that the injury was not, in fact, complete—the cord was not completely severed.

Blake Mealer

Brock's older brother

When Brock got the diagnosis, I didn't think too much about whether or not he was going to walk again. I focused more on what I could control, and that was doing what I could to be there for him. When he was at the hospital in Toledo, we stayed at a place nearby that was like a hotel for the families of the patients. Brock would call me in the middle of the night, and I'd go over to his room so he wasn't by himself. Sharing some encouragement or sleeping in the La-Z-Boy in his room were the best ways for me to support him.

My fiance, Molly, who is now my wife, came with me a lot too. She helped by managing and updating the online care pages to help people know about how he was doing and share his progress.

I didn't have an appetite at all during the first couple of days of recovery. Nothing sounded good to me, but the doctors and nurses kept telling me I needed to eat. Three days after Christmas, I went into another surgery so they could finally fix my broken arm. I was left with a huge cast that ran halfway up my bicep and down to my hand.

All I had was my left arm and my mind. As grateful as I was to have a healthy mind, it was incredibly difficult to feel anything but frustration. I remember hearing all the machines beeping at night and the distinct scent of bleach wafting through the air as I lay there staring at the tile ceiling.

I would randomly feel a wave of pain pass by for what seemed like no apparent reason. Occasionally, I would struggle to lift my head and dip my chin down to look at my legs. I fought to move them, wiggle a toe, or twitch a muscle in my thigh. My tears would blur my vision and trick me into thinking I saw the slightest movement, but it wasn't real. So many simple things I had taken for granted for so long were suddenly ripped away from me.

My only moments of joy at the hospital came from seeing the people I loved and having those few moments of being able to pretend things were okay. I was so miserable, but at the same time, I felt like I should keep those thoughts and feelings to myself. So many people walked into the room with tears in their eyes, and I didn't want to make them walk out feeling worse because of something I said.

Elliott Mealer

Brock's younger brother

I was a senior in high school when we were in the accident, which was only a few weeks after my dad and I talked about my staying with Michigan. We lost my girlfriend, Hollis, and our dad that night. I knew our lives had changed forever.

I remember when they brought us all into a room in Toledo and Brock was lying there, probably in a state of shock, not saying much. I was there with our mom; our oldest brother, Blake; and his wife, Molly. The doctor said Brock was going to go into surgery. We were told he was going to have a one-percent chance of ever walking again. I remember my mom was screaming in disbelief...

I was torn between wanting him to walk again and just making sure he was going to live through it all. I'll never forget sitting there feeling so helpless.

GOD, FAMILY, AND FRIENDS

A wave of relief washed over me when my best friend, Tyler, arrived. His visit was different. With Tyler, I knew I could let my guard down. I asked him for a favor, and of course, he replied, "That's what I'm here for, buddy. Just let me know what you need." That was all it took.

As the tears rolled down my face, I began to be honest with him. I told him about the pain I was in and that the medication didn't seem like it was ever enough. I shared the weird sensations I kept feeling in my legs and how I was trying to understand how they could feel like that as I looked at them lying perfectly still in front of me.

It was terrifying to consider the next wave of sensations I was going to experience—with one leg feeling like it was in the air and the other behind my back, both of them twisted together in a knot, or even what they'd feel like when they suddenly flung themselves the other way to straighten back out again.

I remember telling him I didn't know how I was going to continue day after day like that. Tyler squeezed my hand, wishing he could do something. Then we did the only thing we could do. We prayed.

Deep down, I knew my only hope of getting through that time would be with God and my friends and family sustaining me. I couldn't imagine how or when, but I still wanted to believe that God would find a way forward for me. And not only would I make it through, but He would make a prosperous and happy future for me. I couldn't imagine what it would look like, but my heart still held hope.

When I had some time alone between visits, Tyler came in to let me know that he went to the local television station to make a way for me to watch my dad's funeral from the hospital room. I cried once more as I nodded. The thought of not being with everyone who had been so supportive of my family during our time of grief was overwhelming. It also hurt to recognize that everyone who cared about me would be there, leaving me to agonize over the idea of asking someone to watch it with me from my hospital room instead of being there themselves.

Later that same day, I was visited by my ex-girlfriend's parents. As we talked, it dawned on me that they might be able to be with me during the funeral. It was hard for me to ask them such a huge favor given the past events, but when

I finally asked just before they left, they both nodded in agreement.

On the day of my dad's funeral, my friends at the local television station had set up the television broadcast, but I wasn't able to see much. As the music played, I started to cry. One of my friends from high school played guitar and sang as the pastor and others came up to speak between songs. My tears blurred most of the event, as I broke down having to once again face the agonizing truth that my dad had passed. I was so grateful to have the support of the couple who was there for me that day, holding my hands and crying along with me.

Sandy Barber

Brock's aunt

After the funeral, Brock was in the hospital, and his mom, Shelly, spent a lot of time there. I tried to go up every week and visit with Brock so Shelly could go home and take care of some responsibilities.

Not once when I spent time with Brock did I ever see him upset or worried. He always had a smile on his face. He would say, "Aunt Sandy, I'm going to get through this."

And I said, "I know you are, Brock. You have a lot of determination, and you will!"

MY FIRST SIT-UP

Nearly five days after the accident, two of my nurses came into the room and asked if I would like to sit up. Until this time, I was only able to lean toward my left side with pillows under my right side or to lie flat on my back. I couldn't wait to sit up again!

My excitement was fleeting, however. I watched one nurse carry my legs to one side as the other slid my shoulders so I was lying across the middle of the bed. The nurse by my shoulders gently pushed me up while the other one slowly let my legs down over the edge.

As we went along, they asked if everything felt okay. My back did, which was what I thought mattered, but my legs and body felt miserable. My legs felt hot, and they stung. My abdomen felt as sore as it had ever been.

I immediately noticed a simultaneous feeling of lightheadedness and a headache as I started to rise. Before I even realized it, we stopped, and I was finally sitting up. I moved my eyes around to get a better look around the room, then slowly turned my head left and right. I cracked a slight smile because I was finally sitting up, although each nurse held a shoulder to keep me there.

Sweat started to drip down my forehead, and I noticed that I was out of breath from the exertion, feeling as though the weight of my body was more than I could handle. My mom wanted a picture, so each nurse stepped back with one of them still holding my knees, and I smiled for that brief moment. After the flash, I started to slowly fall back and was asked if I was ready to lie down as the nurses gently pressed me back up. That was an easy yes for me!

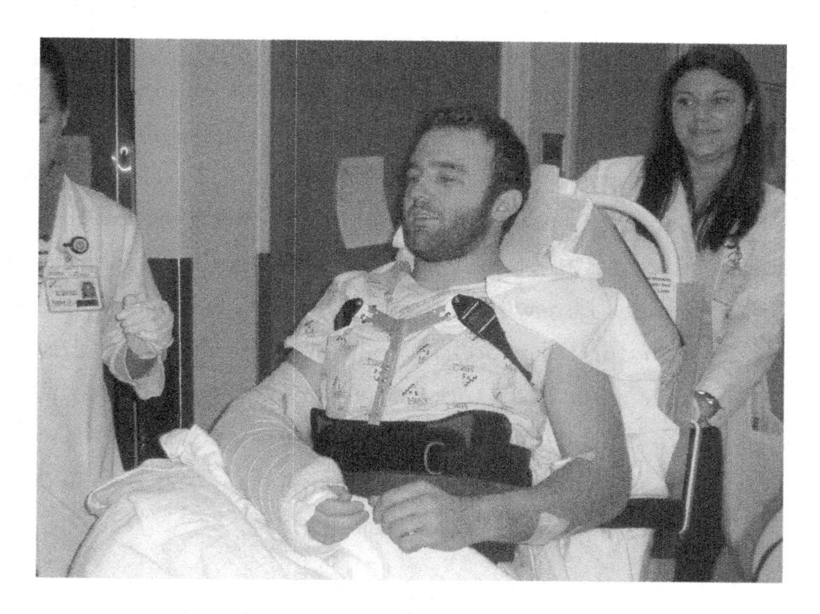

Along with a cast on my right arm, we were very careful about making sure I wore a brace to help support my back whenever I sat up following surgery.

As I lay back on my bed, it felt much more comfortable than before. It was a specially designed air mattress that could be set to various levels of softness. At that moment, it felt perfect. I wiped away some of the perspiration from my face, feeling accomplished, yet I couldn't help but think about how difficult the last several minutes had been.

The back of my mind was trying to figure out how I would ever walk again, especially if sitting up on my own was such a challenge. I couldn't comprehend a road map for that in my mind, so where would I even start? Luckily for me, my mom and my brother Blake helped me gain some clarity on where I was heading.

They told me that I would need to go to another hospital for treatment and physical therapy once I was off my pain medication. They did some research and found a list of the best places to handle spinal cord injuries. At number three was the University of Michigan.

For me, that made perfect sense. First of all, it was close to home, so friends and family members could make a trip up to visit. Secondly, I knew Elliott would soon be there to continue his academics and play football, and I would be able to see him.

After the accident and losing our dad and Hollis, he decided to do the extra required work in high school so he could leave for college early. I had no question that I wanted to go there; I just didn't know when.

Elliott

I was recruited to play football for the Michigan Wolverines by the head coach Lloyd Carr and his staff during my junior year of high school. When I visited, I fell in love with the campus and the coaches, and I really, truly felt a spiritual connection to Michigan. But along with the rest of my family, I was a die-hard, lifelong Ohio State fan, so it didn't quite make logical sense when I felt like God was pulling me toward playing for "our biggest rivals."

But I listened to that small voice, and I made my decision to play wearing the blue and maize. I got made fun of on recruiting websites, with headlines like, *"Player Says God's Telling Him to Go to Michigan,"* and even I knew how ridiculous it sounded.

Then, in November of my senior year of high school, Lloyd Carr announced his retirement, and things seemed to unravel a little bit. Schools started to recruit me again, even though I had committed my junior year and was supposed to officially sign in February of my senior year. Illinois in particular got really aggressive. As a recruit, it made me wonder if I should reconsider. The competing coaches made a good point by reminding me that Michigan would bring in all new coaches that I wouldn't even know.

But then my dad stepped in. He reminded me that I had given my word, so by that fact I was going to Michigan, and I wasn't going to entertain other options. This wasn't an argument by any stretch of the imagination but just who my dad was. The Mealer boys grew up knowing we never backed out of a commitment. And besides, Michigan would be a great school for me. It didn't matter who the coaches were going to be. I was supposed to be there, which was why I verbally committed in the first place.

At the time, I thought it was because I was going to become an NFL star. But in hindsight, I recognize God had a plan that was so much bigger than football. I can look back and see all the amazing connections that happened because I was there.

Before Elliott committed to Michigan, our family was made up entirely of Ohio State fans.

Blake Mealer

Brock's older brother

I remember being such a die-hard Ohio State fan that in eighth grade, I had said that even if Michigan was the only school to offer me a full scholarship to play for them, I still wouldn't go there. But later, when my brother Elliott got recruited by them, I had a change of heart and decided maybe it was a pretty good school after all. If someone would have told me my little brother would play for Michigan, I'd have told them they were crazy, but clearly there was a bigger plan happening that we didn't even realize at the time.

I had to go without the strong pain meds they ran into my IV for twenty-four hours in order to make the trip. Of course, that very evening, I struggled to go without medication. I thought if I could just make it through the night, the next morning I could be on my way to recovery, but that night became the most painful since the accident.

After the sun went down, I remember struggling to say my pain level was okay. I would tell them it was at level three or four when it might have been seven or eight in reality. Tears started running down my face. I knew I couldn't make it and move on. I would be stuck for another day if I gave in.

I finally broke down in the early morning hours, when once again my legs felt crossed and tied up. I touched my left leg with my hand, but somehow, in my mind, I felt as though my right leg was there. Even when I would look down, I couldn't seem to believe my legs were in the right position.

I even had the feeling I was sitting with my legs crisscrossed as I was lying down on my back, petrified that I would have to feel them being pulled apart in an instant. When I gave in to needing the pain medication that night, I felt as though I had failed.

The next day I was given a pick-me-up by getting to do some physical therapy. For me, this meant sitting on my own again. I was transferred into a wheelchair and taken down to a physical therapy area. It felt great just to get out of my room for a while and get the chance to do something other than lie down.

I was greeted by a therapist whose beautiful, genuine smile was rejuvenating. While I'd seen the smiles of countless visitors, hers was glaringly different. This stranger seemed delighted to work with me on my first venture outside my room. I was in high spirits in a new environment. I was moved out of my wheelchair and onto a table where I was able to sit with some help for an entire minute. It felt great to be sitting again, but it was hard to see my legs dangling off the table and knowing I was unable to move them by myself.

The therapist moved them for me after I lay down. I watched as she gently moved my feet and pushed my legs up into a bent position. It was the first time my legs moved that much without hurting. I couldn't feel anything, but somehow it felt good to just get them moving around. The hour or so took a lot out of me. When I arrived back to my room, I couldn't believe how tired I felt.

That afternoon I had a long, much-needed nap.

SETTLING IN AT U OF M

Fortunately for me, after some afternoon visits, I was still feeling good and had completely forgotten about needing pain medication at night. I didn't realize that I had gone without it until the next morning when they notified me that we could schedule a transport. I would leave for Michigan as long as I could continue to go without the meds. My transport was scheduled right after the weekend, around noon on Monday, January 7. I would finally get the chance to gain some independence and figure out what potential I would have for the future.

My ride to Ann Arbor was no picnic in itself. I felt great excitement about getting to move locations and the potential for great progress. At the same time, each bump in the road sent pain through my torso, reminding me of just how bad off I was.

I remember how the driver and the man riding in the back with me kept me smiling by keeping the conversations going. Whether talking about Elliott going to Michigan or how much better I was now than when I arrived at St. Vincent, talking to them did a lot to keep my spirits up.

We arrived at the University of Michigan hospital around two in the afternoon. I was taken up to what seemed to be a nearly empty sixth floor of the hospital. Shortly after I reached my room, an extremely happy and friendly redheaded woman came into my room to announce that she had chosen me as a patient.

I was certainly surprised I was *chosen* but was glad that I would be taken care of by someone so cheerful. She told me her name was Christy and that she would be my number-one nurse. If she was working, she'd be taking care of me.

I had some great nurses at St. Vincent as well, but the big difference seemed to be that I was getting better now that all the other complications I dealt with due to the severity of my injuries were finally out of the way. Christy went on to pepper me with a bunch of questions, some medical and some just general. She also gave me a brief overview of my schedule, which seemed to be very busy, and that was great!

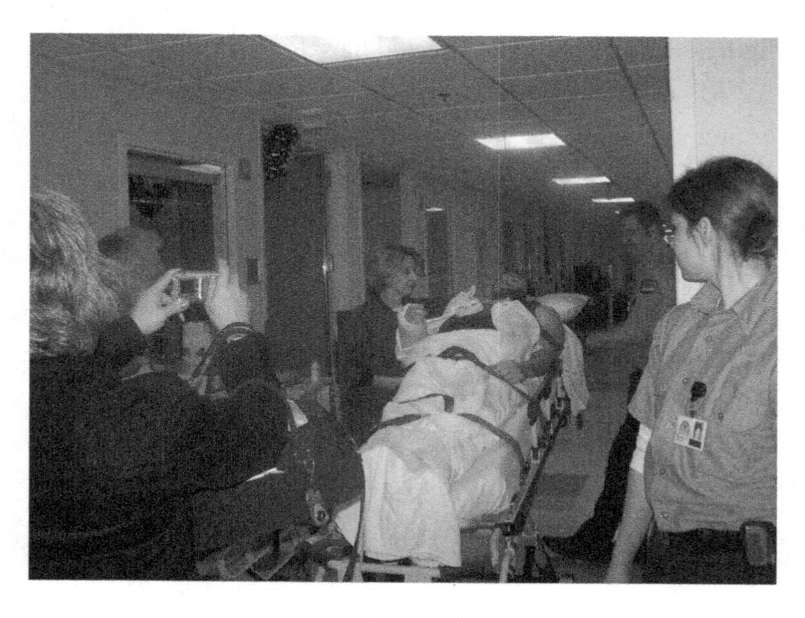

The day I was finally being transferred from St. Vincent's in Toledo, headed for the University of Michigan Hospital.

Blake

I remember the nurses we had in Toledo and the way that they were like little rays of sunshine coming in, looking to help in any way they could. From my perspective, I was always impressed with the way that their day-to-day job was seeing people on their worst days and they still could be able to be positive or uplifting to the families and their patients. They saw such bad things happening, and they were still willing to do their job with kindness.

My day at the U of M Hospital typically began with breakfast. Around six in the morning, there'd be knocks at the door and voices repeatedly yelling, "BREAKFAST!" I would wave an arm, "Thank you," and then continue to sleep until eight.

Once I had really woken up, I would watch TV as I ate my cereal, eggs, and bacon. At around nine, I would get lifted with a harness, pulled over, and lowered into a power chair. I would ride down to the second floor of the hospital for physical therapy and have forty-five minutes of stretching, sitting up, and having my legs moved around.

I would then go down the hall for another forty-five minutes of occupational therapy, where we would talk about how I would live my life and do things on my own after leaving the hospital. I would repeat this routine after lunch, and sometimes I'd be able to go to recreational therapy and play video games or board games to distract myself from the day's struggles.

BACK AND FORTH

The last thing I want you to think is that I was constantly in a positive state of mind during this time. The truth is, I had to work hard to put some practices into place to get myself back into the right mindset over and over again.

Before the surgeon's bleak "one-percent chance" diagnosis, it never really crossed my mind that I wouldn't be able to walk and get back to my pre-accident self. I knew I couldn't feel my legs, but I had just chalked it up to shock until I heard the news from the surgeon. There were moments when I felt like I was looking through her while the words coming out of her mouth sounded like the teachers in the *Peanuts* cartoons ("waa, wa, waa, waa, wa"). It took a lot of time to process that I had a spinal cord injury and was paralyzed.

I teetered between two extreme thoughts:

My life is over.

And ...

Somehow, God's going to heal me. I'll wake up and be 100 percent again. It'll all be over, and I'll never have to think about it again.

It wasn't until the day my nurses helped me sit up that I began to realize the full extent of my injury. My core muscles were so weak I couldn't keep my balance. If the nurses weren't holding me up, I would have collapsed back onto the bed.

I would think, *I'm going to walk again.* And almost immediately, my next thought would be, *How in the world could you walk again when you can't even sit up on your own?*

My mom was in the room with me most of the time, and I think we both tried very hard to put on a brave face for each other while internalizing what was really going on, not wanting to add to the other's burdens. I know in those early days, there were times when she'd ask about my pain, and I'd give her a much lower number, trying to smile and tell her I was doing good.

Each morning I did my best to list the things I was grateful for in my mind. And then I'd go through what I called my morning ritual. I remember getting super excited about getting Frosted Flakes for breakfast instead of some other kind of cereal.

More than half the time, I'd have what I would consider to be a good day, and the rest were terrible. I counted it a terrible day if I puked or soiled myself at physical therapy among other things. We'd do stretching, and sometimes I'd feel a burning sensation down my legs. I'd be sweating profusely and feel light-headed. Then I'd get into a slump after being exhausted and feeling so dragged down. But I'd tell myself I could reset overnight and try to get excited for the potential in a new day.

I created a nightly prayer routine, and I'd repeat different mantras in my head over and over. I'd say things like, *Tomorrow's going to be much better. Today was terrible; tomorrow has to be better. You made it through today, so you can make it through anything. God has a plan. He's got something I don't understand that's coming. It's right around the corner, and I just have to be patient.*

Then my pendulum would swing the other way, and I'd think: *Why did I have to survive? Why was I the one who had to deal with the loss and this injury? Why was I chosen to suffer? What was my sin that caused me to have to pay for it like this?*

Then came the big questions to God: *When will I be healed? Why haven't You done anything? Where are You?* I was mad at Him. In those dark moments, it felt clear to me that He wasn't there at all.

There were times in the middle of the night when my mom was asleep that I'd sit in silence like a monk and say, *Okay, God. This would be a great time for You to send me a sign that everything is going to work out.*

I just wanted to see any kind of proof that He was listening. It could have been something as little as a pen falling off a shelf. I just wanted any kind of a sign. And I'd wait. And watch. And nothing happened. It was easier to cry about my situation at night. When my distress woke my mom up, I'd just shrug it off and tell her I had a nightmare.

THE WEIGHT OF THE WORDS

If you think about it, the accident was less than twenty-four hours prior when my surgeon gave me a one-percent chance of ever walking again. It might make you wonder why she would say such a thing before letting all the swelling go down or giving me some time to heal before sharing an opinion. It might bring up some feelings that she was just being negative or that it wasn't fair. You may be wondering what in the world she was thinking by feeding me such a limiting perspective.

But let's look at it from her point of view. She wasn't just looking at X-rays. She opened me up and got to see it all firsthand. Part of the reason the surgery took so long was because two vertebrae were so shattered as a result of such a hard, traumatic hit. She had the experience of thousands of other surgeries to compare mine to, and it didn't look good, to say the least.

It makes me think of those movies when a kid meets a baseball player and the pro looks at them and says something to the effect of, *You're never going to be me. You don't have what it takes to get to this level.*

The words we hear from others and the thoughts that show up in our minds carry a lot of weight. And we need to decide what we want to pick up and own versus what we can set down and leave behind. For me there was always this little voice in the back of my mind whispering, *This is only temporary.* Some days I fully believed it, and others I had to fight to hear it. But in the end, that voice was the one that helped me keep moving forward.

Aunt Sandy

Not only did Brock's family stand by him, but the whole community did.

Everyone wanted to help. I received so many calls from people.

"How is he doing?"

"What can we do to help?"

No matter where any of us were during that time, someone was stopping and saying, "We're praying for you. . . we're praying for Brock. . . we're praying for your family."

WHERE ARE YOU?

Maybe you're at a crossroads moment in your life. You could think you're on the verge of your rock bottom. You might have already hit it and are ready to start climbing your mountain again. Or you could be making good progress without fully knowing what the next step is that would get you closer to breaking through the clouds to finally see the peak.

It took years for me to be able to look back at this time and realize that God was definitely with me in those dark moments. Now I'm at a place in my life where I'm able to see the "God things" so much more easily than before.

Along the way, I was blessed to have people reminding me that I was so close to the next little milestone, and it helped me to keep trying. My mom was there with me every day, and I was so grateful to have her enthusiasm for each little thing when it felt like there wasn't much to get excited about.

But when I had visitors who hadn't seen me in a while reminding me of the progress I'd made since the last time they saw me, it was a huge boost. I don't think a lot of us are wired to remind ourselves about where we were a few days, weeks, or even months ago and compare that to where we are right now. I wasn't intentionally asking people about my progress. It was just the gift of an observation due to the situation I was in.

If you can get into the habit of taking a minute to reflect in that way, it can really help you instead of just thinking about how far away you are from the end goal—even if you have to start by looking at your negative thoughts from an hour ago and the way you gave yourself something positive to focus on instead.

In order to move further up the mountain you're facing, it's important to take inventory of your current situation. You need to be able to reflect on where you are so you can decide how you want to approach what's next.

I know journaling has helped me regain some positivity at different seasons in my life. That is why I'm offering you the opportunity to solidify your thoughts at the end of each chapter from here on out.

Wherever you are, I'd like to invite you to grab something you can take notes on and do some journaling. Be honest with yourself as you consider the following questions:

- How are you feeling on a pain scale of 0 (none) to 10 (excruciating)? This can be physical, emotional, or a combination of the two.
- Are the majority of your thoughts negative or positive?
- What are some routines you can put into place when the negativity is overwhelming?
- What are the things you would say if you had my best friend, Tyler, there to just hear it all?
- What are some positive mantras you can create?

It may be helpful to come back to your responses often as a reminder of the back-and-forth motion you're experiencing. One day you can come back to what you've written as a record of the progress you've made over time.

CHAPTER 3

PROGRESS, NOT PERFECTION

Four days after I arrived at the University of Michigan Hospital, I was finally able to say I had zero pain without any medication. As if this wasn't enough good news for me, I also made progress in physical therapy. My physical therapist (PT) was known as the toughest of all the PTs, and we were told she would push me to my limits. After two weeks of not being able to move or feel my legs post-surgery, she was able to feel some twitching as I tried to squeeze my legs together.

I couldn't see any movement, but she told us it was nearly unheard of to have any muscle response so early after my type of injury. I was considered an incomplete injury but classified as an ASIA B. The ASIA score is used to assess the severity of an injury. An ASIA A is a complete injury with no feeling or movement, and ASIA B is an incomplete injury without feeling or movement. She cautioned us that while it was a positive sign, it certainly didn't guarantee any level of recovery. We were still thrilled to have just the slightest bit of good news that day.

At occupational therapy, I continued to try to keep my hands working. My occupational therapist (OT) had an encouraging spirit and always made it easy to want to accomplish whatever the challenge of the day was. Many times I would have to try figuring out how to do tasks with just my left hand. This wasn't too difficult, as I had always tried to eat left-handed just to get better, but writing was certainly not easy. I tried to write with my right hand, but I decided I would struggle less and be more sloppy with writing with my left hand for now. I also had to practice putting tiny screws into a board with pre-drilled holes with both my left and right. My right hand took a minute or two longer, having to move from my shoulder, back and forth.

I could tell most of the feeling in my right fingers had gone numb, so even picking up the screws was a difficult task. I kept my motivation up and was looking forward to the weekend, hoping there would be more visitors to lift my spirits.

The first weekend didn't disappoint. I had visitors come throughout Saturday and Sunday. I was still able to do some physical therapy on both days, and people had the opportunity to come along or stay with me as I stretched and worked in my room.

Being blessed with so many visitors made the weekends fly by, and even the weekdays seemed to pass quickly. The nights, on the other hand, felt endless. As soon as the lights went out, there was no way to rest my mind. My thoughts raced, going back to the month that had just gone by, and feelings of sorrow overcame me.

Hours would pass, and as it just seemed I was falling asleep for the first time, there would usually be a nurse who would stop in to take blood. As the soreness of yet another blood draw would subside, I would hear someone shout, "Breakfast!" But I tried to continue getting up each morning prepared for something good to happen, no matter how little rest I had the night before.

My first big milestone came on January 16, just a couple of weeks after arriving in Michigan. After seeing the twitches the week before, I was laid on my side, with my top leg on a short table. My PT laid a cotton sheet underneath the leg. With a bent knee, I was told to try and straighten my leg out.

I stared at the mirror in front of me, watching my leg as I suddenly kicked it. It moved one or two feet! The PT would pull it back, and I would kick again. My mom and I were ecstatic as she sat across the table from me, witnessing kick after kick. We knew a prayer had been answered just to be able to see something new happen. I finally had a glimpse of something positive I could build on.

I tired quickly after just ten or so kicks with my left leg, so we switched. My right leg was slow to start and was not sliding quite as strongly as the left. The excitement from moving my left leg was enough to keep me from feeling disappointed though. Somehow I knew the right leg would come around with time.

Some of the other therapists had seen our excitement and came to see what had happened. Some just smiled; others seemed to have watery eyes. I was just as excited to share some good news with everyone else as I was for myself.

I reflected on that night, and I was proud of the day I had put in. But I also dealt with more pain than usual as I tried to sleep. I tossed and turned, having physical pains adding to my typical emotional ones.

The next morning my brother Elliott came by to visit. He was on his way to have surgery on his shoulder. I knew his shoulder was injured in the accident and was only told that it would be okay after surgery.

It wasn't until sometime later that my mom told me he had actually torn his rotator cuff while trying to lift our vehicle back to the upright position to help get me out. At the time I had no idea that was the case. It would have only added to the overwhelming emotions I felt.

Finding out later simply allowed me to accept the action as a powerful act of love, not just his concern for me, but his lack of concern for himself in that moment of immediate need. The goals and aspirations he had worked so hard for were put on hold without a thought because he felt he had to do something the night of the accident.

Elliott's surgery went well, and after we greeted him coming out of surgery, he headed home to rest. I was glad to be able to sit down and talk to Elliott briefly and share the small steps of progress we had made since being injured. We both encouraged each other to keep getting better, and I had to continue with physical therapy after he left for home.

In my next session, I was feeling excited to get the chance to move my legs again. As I sat on the mat in the PT room, my legs dangled just inches from the ground. I tried to kick or move them as they hung—but I couldn't.

I initially felt disappointed, but I was reinvigorated when I had the chance to move them on the table again.

I showed some new visitors my progress, and then I had to move on to a new challenge—squeezing my legs together. I tried to use the same method to bring my legs together that I had used to kick them, but I couldn't get any immediate results. I realized that patience was always my most valuable asset, but it never came easily.

HIGHS AND LOWS

I was excited on the day I was finally able to get the staples removed from my arm. I was somewhat concerned at how that would feel, but I was relieved to feel it was relatively painless. The scrubbing stung as I felt a combination of numbness and a pins-and-needles sensation while they cleaned it.

The disappointment came from seeing my arm nearly as slender as the bone itself and learning a new cast would imprison it after less than twenty-four hours in a splint. It would still be a few more weeks before I could even begin to have my right arm back. In the meantime, I knew I would have to continue to try to do everything I could with just one arm.

On the morning of Monday, January 22, I was optimistic and ready for more progress once again. I had a therapist I hadn't worked with before that day, which was always interesting. I pulled my power chair up to the mat, parked it, and used my arms to place my feet on the ground until the PT was ready to help me get onto the mat. I made a simple mistake that day, forgetting to turn the chair to the Off position while I was parked. The PT came over and lifted the arm of the chair up so I could move to the mat. As the arm reached the chair back, the power chair started moving forward, and I heard my mom scream as the PT quickly lowered the arm.

I sat in confusion as the PT called for help. Then I realized everyone was looking at my feet. I felt a slight tingle as I lowered my eyes, only to see my left foot was behind the front tire, with my toes pointed directly to my left. At first, it made me sick to see my foot in such an abnormal position, but I immediately turned my thoughts to an appreciation that I couldn't feel it at the moment. I casually raised my head, thinking to myself, *That looks like it really hurts.*

They carefully rolled the chair back, and one PT helped guide the front tire. I lay on the mat as they examined the foot, coming to the consensus that it was okay. With that I continued on with my normal workout that day, leaving behind any thoughts of using the incident as an excuse to call it a day.

When I got back to my room, I found a small but heavy package waiting for me. Who doesn't love to receive a package, especially one that is a complete surprise? I was curious as to why it was so heavy, and then I found an envelope inside.

Even the envelope itself was heavy, and as I unfolded it, a gold medal fell into my lap. It had a hand holding a torch on the front, and it was encircled by the words "Goodwill Games."

The letter inside was from one of Elliott's high school football teammates, Clay Simpkins, the kicker. He told me that he had gone to Mexico for the Goodwill Games to compete in several karate competitions. He won silver for his first routine and then had to take on a three-time champ in the weapons routine. He said that as he was about to begin, he thought about my situation and the attitude I chose, believing I would walk again someday.

He said he felt so inspired that he went through his routine like clockwork and had never performed it so well before. The letter moved me to tears, thinking that someone would send the award they had worked so hard to achieve in the mail to give me back the inspiration I had shared with them. It gave me much-needed fuel to get back to work day in and day out.

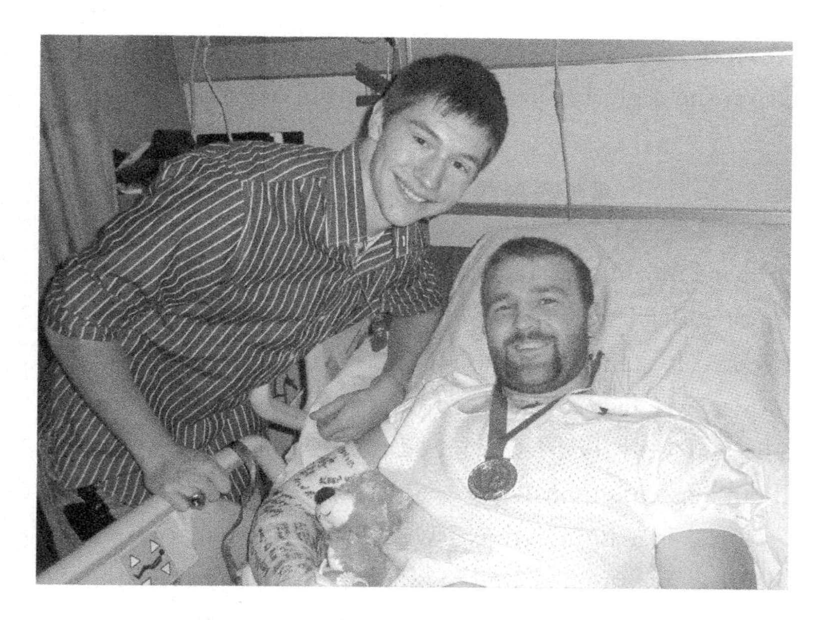

Clay Simpkins, Elliott's friend from high school, came to visit me shortly after returning from the Goodwill Games.

As my days turned into weeks at the hospital, I started to realize I hadn't shaved. My beard had grown quite thick, and the nurses started to ask if I was growing it out. I told them it wasn't the plan, but I might as well since my shaving hand was on a break. I felt the look suited me well enough, so I decided to keep it throughout my hospital stay. When I saw myself in the mirror, I could tell I looked different. I had never grown my beard this thick, and I didn't know if I liked it.

Beard aside, I worried that I had become a different man after the accident and wondered if I would like the person I saw in the mirror. Would I become someone else through all this? Would I be a better man or a flawed version of myself? Thinking about the long-term future made me worry more than dream, so I tried to keep my sights set on progressing from the night before to the beginning of each morning.

STANDING AT LAST

On the morning of January 25, I was given the choice to do my regular leg exercises or to try to stand up. Of course, I wanted to stand up. I was laid onto a mat and then strapped down. My feet were placed on a plate at the lower end of the mat, and then I was raised up, feeling an awful lot like Frankenstein's monster.

The mat hummed as I was slowly tilted to twenty-five degrees. We stopped, and my PT asked how I was feeling. So far so good, so we continued up to about forty-five degrees. It felt different for sure, but I wasn't feeling too bad, so we slowly continued to work our way up until I was finally standing.

I took a look around the PT area. I had a whole new perspective on things. I was finally up at eye level, able to get a seemingly bird's-eye view of things. We were able to undo the top couple of straps to free my upper body, and I slowly leaned forward and back as far as I could. It only took a few of those before I started to sweat and feel a little queasy, so I lay back down.

The next week in OT, I was placed in a standing frame. It puts more of the weight on the legs, and you are lifted up similar to the way a jack lifts up a car. Each pump of the lever would raise my butt up and over my knees, until I was upright, with a clear plastic tray in front of my arms.

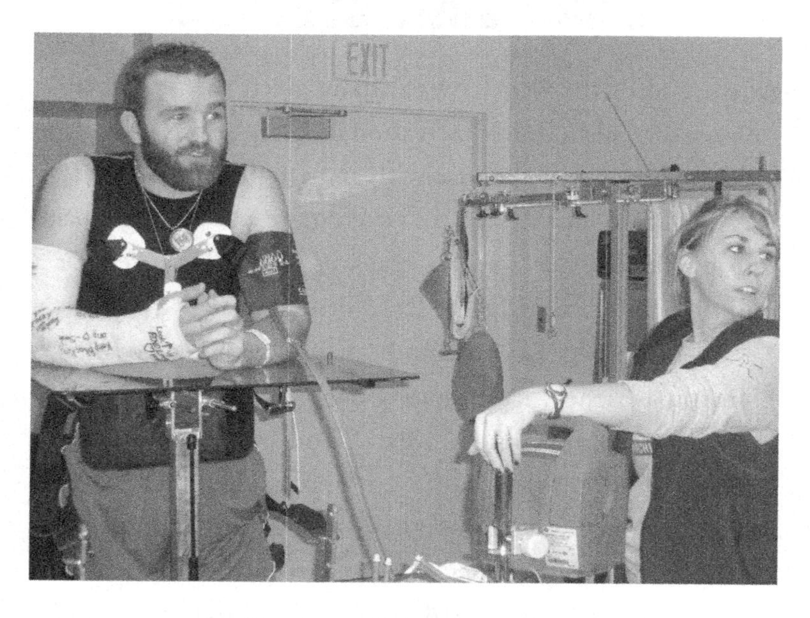

Jamie, my occupational therapist, would often engage me in conversation or a board game to keep me distracted from how uncomfortable it was standing in a frame.

While I stood, we played a game of cards to keep me occupied. As I tried to think about my next card in a game of Go Fish, I quickly felt lightheadedness set in. Sweat started to drip down my face as my OT asked how I was doing. We were about eight minutes in, so we decided to stop the card game and just try to breathe and make it to the ten-minute mark. I was relieved to sit back down, but I felt like I had been knocked down a few pegs since I was only able to stand for ten minutes. At the same time, it was a new milestone and something I could build on next time.

SUPER BOWL SURPRISE

At the end of the week, I was finally given the opportunity to leave the hospital. My recreational therapist was giving me a ride to eat at a steakhouse with some family and friends. I was excited about the food, but even more excited to get back into public life, having felt like I was institutionalized for a month, enough to make me feel a little stir-crazy.

I was joined by my mom, Elliott, and a couple of hometown friends. I thoroughly enjoyed my sirloin steak, a big step up from the usual hospital food I had to eat. As hard as it was getting lifted into a van and maneuvering around the restaurant, I was just happy to see that it could be done.

I had hoped that I would be able to go out on February 3 for the Super Bowl as well, but I realized that wouldn't be possible with the logistics of scheduling a ride, having help, and my new understanding of how much an outing drained me. I had no idea at that time that staying at the hospital for the Super Bowl would be the best decision I could've made and would be crucial toward where my future would lead.

As I sat up in my hospital bed wasting time before the Super Bowl kickoff, my mom came into my room with a big smile on her face. She told me I had a visitor and needed to get out of bed.

This was peculiar since I usually just tried to rest when visitors would come, but she was insistent as she shifted back out of the room. I decided it must be an important visitor, perhaps even the mystery guest Elliott had kept asking about, so I carefully sat up. The process was still a struggle—pulling my legs off the bed with my left hand, shifting to the side, and then trying to press my butt off the bed onto the sliding board that slid me over to the chair. I always had a sigh of relief once I was in the chair and could wipe the sweat off my forehead before going where I had to go. With perfect timing, my mom came back in with the visitor just behind her.

Having been watching the selection of Michigan's new football coach on ESPN diligently, I immediately recognized Coach Rodriguez when he came into my room. It was shocking to me. Not only was it Super Bowl Sunday, but at the time, he must've been the busiest man in Michigan, having just been selected as the new head coach. I shook his hand (with my uninjured left hand) as he introduced himself and sat down on a chair my mom had pulled out for him to sit across from me.

He asked about my progress, and I felt proud to have such an important guest come to visit *me* of all people. Needless to say, I was enjoying it, as I did all visitors, but I wasn't expecting anything life-changing during our brief visit. But I will never forget what Coach Rodriguez told me.

"Well, it's encouraging to hear that you are making some progress, I know you'll keep getting positive signs if you keep faith and work hard," he said. "In fact, I could see you leading our team out onto the field one day if you keep at it. Whenever you are ready and willing, it would be our honor to have you lead us. I know it can be hard to keep at it with everything you have had to deal with, but just try to focus your energy on getting better. I will do all I can to help along the way."

As he spoke, I thought to myself, *What a wild, ambitious idea to talk about.*

I always wanted to walk again, but it was the first time I really visualized the goal clearly. In this visualization, walking was miraculous, but just one of many incredible pieces of the puzzle. To actually be out there with my brother and the entire football team on a Saturday in the fall at the nation's largest stadium was extraordinary to imagine.

"That means a lot. It is hard to focus with all the worries, but I will remember that. I don't know how I'll get there, or how long it will take, but I will definitely take you up on that."

Coach Rodriguez went on, "You'll get there, and if there is anything else I can do for you, you just let me know."

I mentioned that it would mean a lot to Elliott if he could have the number fifty-seven, the year our dad was born as a tribute to him. He told me to consider it done and to focus on my recovery and my future. As he left, he let me know that I was welcome to visit anytime.

After about thirty minutes of being able to talk with the most talked-about college coach in the country, he told me he was going to let me rest or get back to watching the Super Bowl. I had completely forgotten that it had started during the time he was there. I thanked him for his time, and my mom gave him a huge hug as he left. I was still in awe of having someone of his stature show up in my room. I was certain it was hard enough for him to find time to meet with players, let alone come to visit me.

I was humbled to know that he took the time to see me, even during Super Bowl Sunday when so many people were watching the game. It was clear to see how genuine his concern was while he was there. It inspired me to think that if someone that important, someone who would be helping shape my brother's future, was able to come to visit me, I could certainly have confidence in my goals enough to give it 100 percent.

MEETING MIKE BARWIS

During the next week, I felt sick most of the time, having to return to my room either to vomit or because of a high fever. I continued to try and bounce back each day, slowly getting stronger. On February 7, I was visited by more of Elliott's coaches. The offensive line coach, the wide receiver coach, and the strength and conditioning coach, Mike Barwis, came to visit during the day I was in physical therapy. I remember doing some left arm workouts as they walked in, each coach introducing himself.

They all clearly wanted to come to see me work my butt off, urging me to go through everything with all the effort I had. They asked about the different workouts I was trying to learn and when I'd get rid of my cast. My PT explained some of the workouts, the nature of my injury, how I was going to be able to learn to get in and out of bed on my own, and how I would eventually use a manual wheelchair.

Mike's raspy voice was as memorable as they come, but not as memorable as his motivational spirit. Although I was just doing some simple, seemingly meaningless arm workouts at the time, he somehow made them seem like they were for the world championships.

It didn't take long for Mike to be done with the formalities and begin to show he had a clear purpose in his visit other than to show support.

"So, Brock, when are we going to get you up and walking again?" he asked, glancing at me and my PT, waiting for whoever was willing to answer first.

"I hope it's very soon," I responded. "Right now, I've only been able to stand in a frame, and I usually get too lightheaded to stand very long."

My PT added, "Brock actually has a very serious spinal cord injury, and it is very difficult to say when or if he will recover. With what we know about his injury, walking isn't a very realistic goal."

Mike smirked, "Ah, between you and God, you'll get there. If you want to get started on some real work, come over to the weight room. We'll have you up and walking, working out with the team."

I smiled at the thought. "Ha, and I thought this was hard. I'd love to give it a shot if that's what it takes."

My PT rolled her eyes as she gave me another arm exercise to work on.

But Mike continued, "If you think you're working now, just wait. We'll really put you to work!" He smiled and laughed, rubbing his fist into his palm as he paced back and forth.

My PT chimed in, "Brock *is* working very hard, but in my thirty years of working with spinal cord injuries, I've found the most important thing is to focus on life after the injury. We are getting a wheelchair for him and teaching him to get in and out of bed on his own. It will be much easier for him once he gets rid of that awful cast! But he will get there."

"Well," Mike said, still wringing his hands, "you won't be needing the chair too long once you're out of that cast. Once you come to work with me, you'll be learning to get out of bed on your legs again! You just let me know when you're ready. I can tell you are tough, and you'll find a way to get back on your feet."

The other coaches nodded in agreement and smiled.

SPIRIT-RAISING SUPPORT

After they left, I remember knowing at that moment that Mike was the kind of guy I wanted to follow. My PT reiterated to me I shouldn't listen to people like that; they would only set me up to fail. She told me Mike didn't even know how severe my spinal cord injury was and probably had never even worked with anyone who was paralyzed.

I didn't know if he would be able to "fix" me or if he had any experience, but if he was smart enough (or crazy enough) to believe I would walk again, I wanted to have someone who fully believed it, or just someone who thought I had a one-percent, or even fifty-fifty, chance. I could tell he believed there was a way—*100 percent*. I had the heart, faith, and the will to take on the challenge, as difficult as it was.

Part of what convinced me was realizing how hard it would be to tell someone in my situation that they would walk again the way he did. He had just met me. Unlike my family and friends who knew me and supported me, he didn't know much about me, but he still believed I could overcome my injury.

A part of me was worried, knowing how hard physical therapy was, and wondering, *How much harder would I have to work to walk again?* I knew I would have to get much stronger than I was then, mentally and physically.

The following week, as I was leaving physical therapy to return to my room, I had a phone call from an unrecognized number.

As I answered, the voice on the other end said, "Hello, this is Coach Jim Tressel. Is this Brock?"

I reluctantly decided to play along, answering that it was, wanting to listen further to see if this was simply a prank call from one of my friends. He told me he just wanted to call to express his condolences for our loss but also support for my recovery. As he spoke, I began to realize that it was, in fact, Coach Tressel, the head coach of the Ohio State football team.

After I shared some of my initial progress with him, he asked about how Elliott was doing as well. He told me it was his understanding that I had another quarter of school to finish and told me that I would be welcome to come visit the team whenever I returned, despite knowing I would be cheering for Michigan in the fall. I told him I was very grateful for that and especially for the call. It was a great moment, knowing that I had support from all around and believing more and more that I could overcome the injury.

I had a huge goal in front of me, and with an open mind and Mike's voice ringing in my ears, I was ready to do what it took to start working with him.

NO PLACE FOR COMPARISON

Someone recently gave me a copy of *Green Bananas: The Patrick D. Rummerfield Story*. It's a book about a race car driver who was told he had seventy-two hours to live after breaking his neck in a car crash. The title refers to advice from a childhood lesson given by his dad: *Never buy green bananas unless you plan on being around long enough to enjoy them!* His story goes on to share how he completely defied those seventy-two-hour odds and went through years of intense rehab, eventually becoming a triathlete, setting world endurance records.

The kind of work he had to put in was somewhat similar to mine. I was never given a death sentence, and our injuries were very different, but he pushed himself through grueling workouts to be able to beat the odds and walk again, among other things.

We've all heard the saying, "Comparison is the thief of joy."

I agree. It can be difficult to start comparing your life to someone else's who has "blazed a trail" or done something near the ballpark of what you want to achieve. In the world of spinal cord injuries, we have to start by looking at the nature of the injury—which plays a part in how doctors consider your odds of different types of recovery.

It may feel comforting to hear about someone who has done the thing you want to do, but you have to be careful not to get discouraged. In my case, I heard about people who had injuries and were able to walk again. But at this point in my recovery process, there wasn't anyone in front of me with the exact same injury to measure my progress against.

Getting feedback from visitors was a great help and learning to consciously look back and remind myself of how far I had come since the first day I tried to sit up helped me compare old progress to new progress. And that was enough.

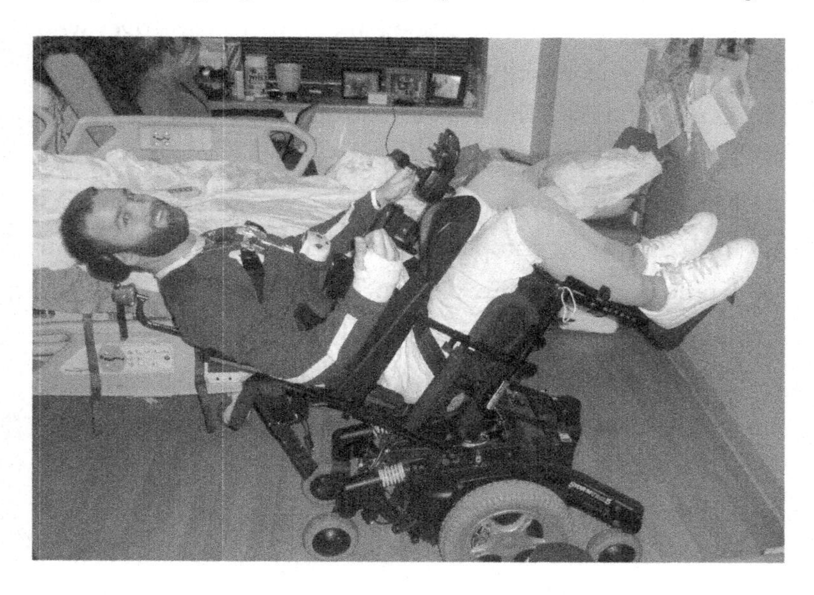

With a still healing right arm, I used a power chair to get around. I would constantly use the tilt feature to help prevent pressure sores from sitting, and at times, for the entertainment of seeing people's reactions!

WHAT IS REALISTIC FOR YOU?

Whenever I think about the word *realistic*, my mind goes to the idea of some of my friends having a bucket list. For the record, I don't have one. But when I look at my life, I see so many different things have happened that never would have made it to a bucket list because when you consider them, they're not realistic at all.

I never would have written down the names of different people I've met or opportunities I've had because they make no logical sense. There's no way some of the encounters I wrote about here would have ever crossed my mind. I would much rather stay open and keep everything on the table while going with the flow, taking each new opportunity as it comes.

To me, the hardest part is pushing yourself by doing something you've never done before. But once you've done it, you already know you can do it one more time, then you can keep doing it over and over.

I know in books and different types of media we often read and hear that our limitations are only in our minds, and if we can just believe, we can make things happen. I've found that, yes, limits are in our minds, but there are also things that are limited by time. Something may be unrealistic for you today, but it isn't necessarily unrealistic for you a year or even five years from now.

Maybe your goal is to dunk a basketball. How much time are you willing to sacrifice to do that? What would you be willing to overcome to have that moment of achievement? If it isn't high on the list of things you want to do in your life, it may not really be worth striving toward.

In college, I got to the point where I just barely could dunk a basketball unencumbered. And if I had enough wishes, I could add it to my list, but at this point in my life, I don't think it's a top priority, so I can easily let it go and focus on other things.

Whether it's dunking a basketball, changing careers, or starting a business, it's all a matter of time and the effort you're willing to put in. And you're ultimately the only one who can make that decision for yourself.

Suppose I would have smiled politely at Mike the day we met and decided he was just trying to be nice but there was no way I'd be able to walk again. Where would I be today if I had latched on to any of the (medically quite valid) excuses that ran through my mind?

BROCK'S RULES FOR GOING AFTER YOUR GOALS

Whenever I think of giving advice to an audience on creating goals, I hear Mike's voice in my head. He has always had a way of saying just what I needed to hear when I needed to hear it the most. I'll share more about my support system and how you can create your own in chapter five, but let's take some time to consider a goal you have and what you can do to keep moving toward it. Grab your journal.

1. **Start by creating the big picture in your mind.** I can still hear Mike painting the picture for me: *You've been to the games, but this time, they'll all be looking at you. As you take your first step and lead the team out, you'll hear the roar of the crowd. The difference that day is that those 110,000 voices will be cheering for you. Your eyes will move from the turf under your feet to the banner and then up to the maize and blue in the stands. Your cheeks are going to be sore from all the smiling, and you'll feel a wave of emotions as you lift your right hand and the crowd gets on their feet to share the moment with you.*

   * Think about your big goal, whether it's personal or professional.
   * Write about the day it comes true like you're sharing a scene from a movie with yourself:
     * Who will be there?
     * How will they react?
     * What will you see?
     * What will you hear?
     * How will you feel?

2. **Acknowledge the baby steps.** Sitting, standing, and kicking my legs were some big and small moments that helped me notice some progress. If I decided that the only time I could be happy was when I walked onto the field, the peak of the mountain would have felt even more impossible to achieve. Remember that each small improvement is moving you up your mountain, and if you

keep doing the things over and over, you'll look back and realize you're further along than you thought.

- Create a list of baby steps to highlight on your way up the mountain:
  - What are some small wins you've already overlooked?
  - What is the next step forward?
  - How do you want to acknowledge your next step?

3. **Choose to belong.** When I chose to work on my MBA, I was surrounded by doctors. And when I was in the gym with Mike, I was in the presence of elite athletes. I could have decided I wasn't worthy or that I didn't fit in, but instead, I embraced the opportunity with gratitude and rose to the occasion.
   - Write about the places your goal will take you.
     - What are the kinds of people you'll interact with?
     - What are their qualifications?
   - Write a note reminding yourself what you'll be doing there, and instead of telling yourself why you don't belong, lift yourself up the way you would a close friend and let yourself know of all the reasons that you believe in yourself.

Looking back at this time of my life, I remember feeling like a little kid with the "grown-ups" talking about me as though I wasn't right in front of them, hearing every single word they said.

There were so many times when I could have just believed that I couldn't make any more progress. I could have agreed that Mike was crazy and just didn't get where my PT was coming from. I could have given any number of valid excuses to never call him or give what Coach Rodriguez said any more thought.

But that's not who God made me to be.

CHAPTER 4

AGREEING TO DISAGREE

As my daily routine became somewhat monotonous, I started to wonder when and how I would ever get out of it and what normal life outside of a hospital would look like. For the time being, I knew I had no control over it, but the uncertainty still bothered me. It didn't help that as I started transitioning into a manual wheelchair, my PT explained it was time I began accepting my situation and moving forward with my new life.

Between stretching and strengthening exercises, I had to practice getting in and out of the wheelchair using my left hand. My mind was set on figuring out *my own way* of getting through challenges, quietly reminding myself that each method would only be a temporary solution until I was more capable and strong enough to find a new, easier way.

One example was trying to get into the wheelchair after being on the ground. My PT told me to first set the brakes and position myself so that I was face down with my head toward the chair. I had to push myself back onto my knees into a four-point stance so that I could reach up to the front of the chair, getting into a kneeling position. From there, I lifted my knees up, twisting as I reached my weaker right hand to the left, and pressed my left fist down as I turned my butt back onto the seat.

It was terribly awkward, and I failed time after time. My knees hit the footplate of the chair, or my feet would tangle, or I couldn't press hard enough to lift myself or get high enough to land on the chair. My frustration led to taking a break so I could calm down.

During that physical rest, I came up with a different way. While I sat with my back against the chair and my legs straight out in front of me, I realized it would be so simple if I could start from that position. I reached up and behind me to the front of the chair, clutching the titanium bars on each side, then pressed down, lifting my butt into the air as I pulled myself back, sliding onto the seat. Even though it took more strength and less finesse, it was much simpler for me.

My PT told me I'd injure my shoulders and break them down by repeating that kind of movement over time, but I knew I wouldn't have to do it for the rest of my life.

As my body continued to heal, my mom continued to press my PT to give me a chance to walk and find a way to get me back on my feet. I kept getting in the standing frame to increase my endurance for being upright. I still got lightheaded as the standing time approached an hour, but it felt amazing to be back at the height I had grown accustomed to. One memorable afternoon, my PT finally gave in and told me we were going to put some braces on my legs, lift me up in the harness, and see how it would go.

THE NEXT ATTEMPT

Putting the braces on was miserable. Even with the little sensation I had, the leather straps seemed to pinch, and the metal bars pressed against my skin. Experiencing what seemed like excessive pain as we tried to adjust the braces into place reminded me that I'd waited too long to let it stop me from trying to walk again. After a long, ten-minute struggle, I was ready to get strapped into a harness and begin my ascent onto my own two legs.

The head spinal cord doctor came to observe that day. I wasn't sure if he came especially for my next attempt at standing or if it was a random drop-in to the PT department (as was pretty common), but either way, it did give me a sense of importance beyond what I had already felt. I convinced myself that the doctor's visit could help him see that I would walk again, and all the people in PT that day were about to see something incredible.

My determination faded after I was standing and then slowly the weight of my body shifted from the harness to my brace-stabilized legs. I could feel the blood rush to my legs, the pressure building as they swelled, and how they pressed even more into the leather straps. I tried to fend off the feeling of lightheadedness as I focused on just trying to take a step.

It was extremely grueling. I couldn't figure out how to even begin. After twenty-four years of walking, just the last two months of not walking seemingly wiped my muscle memory away. I tried to shift all the weight to my left side, which might have been as simple as just leaning my head in that direction. Then I tried to think about pulling my right hip and side forward.

I slowly shifted back to the center and glanced down to see my right foot scoot forward by just a few inches. I shifted my focus to the other side of my body, going through the same process, then glancing down to find my left foot ever so slightly ahead. After going back and forth less than a dozen times, I cracked a smile and realized it was time to call it a day.

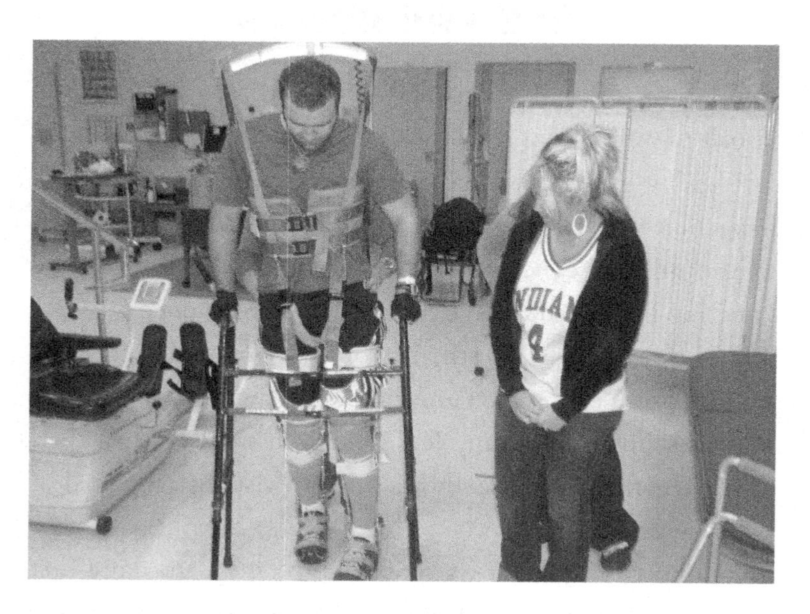

One of the first few days of walking in a harness without the cast on my right arm, with Molly Mealer alongside.

I was thrilled about the progress I just witnessed, but the pain of swollen legs and the lightheadedness quickly overcame the excitement I felt. Even after lying down, I felt exhausted and miserable. My only relief came once the braces were completely off. Then I could finally celebrate a seemingly small yet actually huge victory that day.

The head doctor and my PT congratulated me on having exceeded expectations and proceeded to tell me about a new robotic treadmill therapy that could aid my progress. It was hard to say what would come next for me, but I knew I had to exhaust every opportunity and give my full effort if I was going to live without regrets during this struggle.

UPS AND DOWNS

The Lokomat, as it was called, breathed new life into my efforts to walk again. I wasn't sure what the experience would be like, but I knew it would move me forward. The Lokomat is a machine with robotic legs that can walk paralysis victims on a treadmill. The concept seemed exciting to me, and sometime later, my PT began to take me to the machine once or twice a week for about a month. It wore me out, much like the standing frame, but it felt amazing to see myself in the mirror and look down to see my feet go one in front of the other. It was the first time I really was able to visualize my goal of walking again so clearly.

Although my mom wasn't able to be there the day I first tried to walk, it gave me great joy to be able to call her with the surprising news. I knew I would get the opportunity to show her, but I just wanted to be able to share the experience over the phone. She fully believed I could walk again and wanted me to have the opportunity for so long. When it finally happened, her excitement was evident, even through the phone. I knew there would be a lot of people who would want to come to see me take steps, but I needed the weekend to rest.

A friend from high school, Brett, happened to visit one Thursday and asked if I would like him to come back the following week. I loved having regular visitors and talking about something other than my condition, so I of course said yes. Throughout the last two months of my stay at the hospital, Brett came to visit every Thursday, as did athletes from the Michigan From the Heart program. It meant a lot to me that Brett chose to be there for me, and it gave me a lot of enthusiasm to know I could always count on him to show up.

On one of those Thursdays, a man whom patients knew as "Coach" from Michigan From the Heart and my recreational therapist offered to take me to a hockey game. Of course, I asked Brett if he would come along, and he did. That afternoon the biggest snowstorm of the winter rolled in. Luckily, Brett was already in Ann Arbor, but I was worried we wouldn't even be able to go across town to see the game. The recreational therapist assured me that we would make it there; we just had to leave early and take our time.

It was hard to see out of the van as we drove a couple of miles over the next twenty minutes to Yost Arena for the game, but our driver let us know as we were getting close. I began to notice that anytime I dressed warmly to go outside, I would heat up quickly, sweat, and feel sick, almost like having motion sickness. The same would happen when I went back inside where it was warm after being cold. My body just couldn't adjust to the sudden temperature changes, so it was a relief in more ways than one to get out of the van and into the game.

We were greeted by an usher, and a huge smile came to my face as we entered the arena. People were rushing in all directions, carrying food and drinks, and cheering. I felt great joy finally being able to do something I loved.

The usher asked how I was doing, and I responded that I was happy to be at the game. When she came back with a comment about how sad I looked because of my situation, it caught me off guard. My heart sank, and I let out a heavy sigh as I moved on into the arena. I told Brett that her reaction was a real downer, but he told me not to worry about it, reminding me we were there to have fun.

My spirits lifted as Brett helped push me up the ramp to our seats. We were on the corner, which for some sports wouldn't be preferable, but for hockey, it was perfect. I felt like a VIP right there against the glass and couldn't wait for the game to start. As the pregame clock hit zero and the loud buzzer sounded, my anticipation peaked.

The announcer came on the loudspeaker asking everyone to please rise and remove our hats. I realized the national anthem was about to begin, and my eyes rose to find the flag.

As the song began, tears instantly flowed down my cheeks. In the moments leading up to the game, I left my worries behind; then, with one announcement, my tragedy came back to me. I wiped my tears and tried to refocus on being grateful for just being at the game, but it was no use. As "The Star-Spangled Banner" ended and Brett sat down, I told him I had never even thought of not being able to stand for the national anthem with everyone else.

It really hit me harder than I would have expected, had I expected it at all. He told me I would stand for the flag again someday. I agreed, knowing someday I would get to, and it was important to enjoy the game at that moment—something I really needed after all the work and struggles of the week.

Rob, the recreational therapist, and Jamie, my occupational therapist, joined me for a photo with several Michigan hockey players following the game—my first night away from the hospital.

SHIFTING FOCUS

One day I had an unexpected visit from the doctor who kept an eye on my broken arm. He brought the saw they used to cut off my cast the first time, saying it might be time to finally get rid of it. I knew regaining the strength in my arm would come much faster than it would in my legs, and it would give me some much-needed independence and freedom.

As he began to cut into the cast, my highly sensitive skin could feel an irritating tickle. The cast slowly parting from my skin felt warm, then itchy. As he finally pried apart the cast, what lay underneath revealed an arm that was less than half the size of what I remembered. To me, it appeared to be simply bone wrapped in skin. There was little, if any, muscle to see. The sight was somewhat disappointing and unexpected, but the feeling was minimized by focusing on the opportunity to improve my situation.

With a newfound sense of determination, I went to my first visit with a hand therapist adjacent to where I would go to occupational therapy. She seemed even more excited than I was to get started that first day. She was acting as though having a brand-new hand to work on was the gift she had been waiting for. The other therapists just nodded and smiled at me, as if to say, "Aren't you lucky that she gets to work on your hand?"

At first, it seemed as though these trips would be pampering sessions—rubbing off the dry skin, dipping the hand in wax, and massaging it with some moisturizing lotion. Little did I know, these visits would be far from relaxing.

By the end of the session, the hand therapist told me she wanted to try and loosen my hand up since it had been immobile for so long. I thought the massaging would have done that, but apparently, she wanted to get some more movement in my wrist. At first, it felt weird to have my wrist rotated around, but this quickly turned to uncomfortable, then painful!

She slowly rotated the wrist clockwise, then reversed, and continued by stretching it up and down. I attempted to politely let her know that I didn't want to injure the wrist again, but she assured me she knew what she was doing. I wasn't so sure.

My wrist popped and cracked as she pressed her hand down on my knuckles. Part of me started to think the sound was more discomforting than what I felt. The nerves in my hand and fingers were still very numb from my surgery, but everything in my wrist seemed to be intact judging from all I felt during these sessions. On each visit, she seemed to push more and more. I continued to hope that somehow this would pay off in the future.

Although I had my doubts, I was very fortunate to have what seemed to be the most aggressive of the hand therapists. In addition to slowly getting sensation back and getting rid of the itchy dead skin on my arm, I started to be able to regain the range of motion in my wrist. As the soreness subsided, I was able to try rotating it on my own when I took off the small brace I wore during the day.

Once I saw this progress, it made it a little easier to get through hand therapy visits. During my last day at the hospital, my hand therapist came to my room one last time and tried to get all the pops and cracks out of it before I left. She told me most of the scar tissue should be taken care of and that I would be able to get full dexterity if I kept my hand active. I was grateful for those sessions, realizing that if I hadn't gone through them, I might have never been able to use my right hand as well as I can.

MORE TRANSITIONS

Around the time I finally was without a cast, I started to transition to a manual wheelchair. The hospital had one I could use until my insurance provided me with one of my own. It was purple with gray wheels and had noticeably been used a few times. Still, somehow I felt reluctant to give up my easy-to-drive power chair. It was something I associated completely with being in the hospital, and I would much rather leave the hospital without *any* chair.

I wondered how long I would have to use the manual wheelchair and how long it would take for me to adapt to using it every day.

Would I even be able to do any of the things I wanted to do once I left the hospital?

I convinced myself the manual wheelchair would just be one step closer to my independence and even one step closer to recovery—not a step toward a permanent way of life.

My mom was relieved to see me get a manual wheelchair. At one time my PT had told her that she would need to buy a high-roof, accessible van with a lift so I could get around in my power chair (as it was considerably taller and heavier).

It was also a relief considering all of the times my mom had been told she would have to take care of me for the rest of my life or keep me in an independent living center.

A couple of times, nurses who weren't with me every day would try to convince her to take over their duties. Whether it was giving me a sponge bath, using a catheter, or a number of other things, they told her she would have to do them every day once we left the hospital. Needless to say, I was determined to be able to accomplish these necessary tasks on my own.

I was told that using the bathroom on my own without a catheter would be futile. I heard that my bladder wouldn't work, and even if it did, I wouldn't be able to empty it on my own, which could lead to bladder infections or complications with my kidneys. Needless to say, it was a struggle at first, but by the time I was ready to leave the hospital, I achieved the seemingly impossible and spared my mom and myself the need for catheters at home.

Shelly Mealer-Stamm

Brock's mom

The doctors were telling me that Brock would never walk again. But I just couldn't imagine that as the reality for my son. I'd ask, "God, are You the one putting on my heart that he's going to walk again?" I had to believe it was Him and that He had plans for Brock we couldn't yet fathom.

I talked to God all the time and tried my best not to cry in front of my son. If I felt tears coming, I would leave the room or walk down the hall and say, "You know what, God? You need to show up because we have serious problems here. We're talking about a good kid." And God did show up, every single time. Every. Single. Time.

Whenever I'd speak about Brock walking again, or even recovering to the point of being somewhat independent, his doctors and counselors would say I wasn't handling things well and I was setting him up to go into the deepest kind of depression since I didn't know anything about the human body's limits.

They kept telling us that I needed to practice doing all the things the nurses did for him, including helping with a catheter. I told them I wasn't going to learn how to use these things because Brock wasn't going to need my help. They'd come back with, "No, that's not how this works. On this floor, all the mothers learn how to do it. Because if something were to happen, you would need to know what to do."

"No. Uh-uh. I'm not doing that."

"Okay, then next week, we'll do a test to make sure he can empty his bladder on his own."

And guess what? He passed that test—three times!

A HOME VISIT

A couple of weeks before I was set to leave the hospital, I was able to take my first trip back home. I wasn't prepared for how emotional it would be. Up until then, I convinced myself that someday I could return home and everything would be how I remembered it—mainly, my dad would be waiting for me.

Finally seeing our home again for myself brought me to tears. Our shar-pei, Shaydee, had been waiting for us and came prancing up to the car to greet me the way she always did, only this time with a little extra wag in her tail. I came in through our back patio door, which was luckily only a few inches above the patio.

Once inside, my heart sank when I realized I wouldn't be able to run to my room on the second floor as I always had. My mom assured me she would move everything downstairs for me, but it just hurt to realize I wasn't able to go back to *my* room. On the other side of the house, there were several volunteers from church working in the bathroom next to the garage. I went to say hello to each of them. They had taken our small bathroom out and expanded it by borrowing space from the garage so that I would have a roll-in shower I could use when I was home for good.

The prospect of a new bathroom was such a relief, considering the amount of effort it took just to use the regular bathroom during that first visit at home. My brothers, Blake and Elliott, both had to carry me in, set me on the toilet, then leave me for a few minutes until I was finished, and then carry me back out. It was funny at the time, but I knew it would get very old very fast if it was the only way. I was able to visit with a number of friends from home that day; it was a breath of fresh air to be away from the hospital.

Just before I left to visit home, I was invited to a local church's Easter Sunday service. It was the only way I wanted to spend my Sunday, finally being able to go back to church—and on Easter of all days. The pastor had asked if he could introduce me, and I brought my braces just for that reason. Despite standing with a walker and the braces being extremely difficult, I knew I could share the progress I was making with many of the people who had been praying for me over the last few months. I wanted to at least give them that sight, since I didn't have much to say that day.

One of my close friends was there with me and, after my introduction, helped me stand up. It was just as hard as it was at the hospital, but with the cheers of the crowd, my throbbing pains subsided. Being able to look out to see the familiar faces and those of strangers who had helped by praying for me through my darkest moments touched my heart. It was uplifting to see God's love in that moment, knowing there was something supernatural, even in the struggle of standing that day. I prayed that at that moment, I was seeing just a minor glimpse into what would come in my future.

UNPOPULAR OPINIONS

Back at the hospital, I returned to my usual duties. During physical therapy, my PT told me she needed to speak to my mom about my goals going forward, especially once I was home. She told me that I needed to focus on my life and not waste time trying to walk again.

She continued by explaining that in her thirty-five years of experience, she had seen two kinds of people—those who accepted their injury and got on with their lives after realizing they couldn't walk again and those who spent the rest of their lives trying to walk.

She then shared what she observed about the second kind of people, telling me they eventually realized they had wasted so much time. Life had passed them by, and they gave up on life in its entirety. She didn't want me to head down that road and was worried that with how much my mother pushed me, it would eventually break me once I failed.

I assured her I knew I wouldn't be letting my mother down if I didn't walk, but I simply knew I would walk again. I knew she had heard it time after time, but I had faith that God would lead me where I needed to go, and I believed it was to walk again.

Then she sat with me on the table mat, with the wheelchair in front of us. She told me she wanted me to accept the wheelchair, almost like it was a living thing, and realize it was a part of my life now.

I told her I certainly understood its purpose and how I would use it. I just wasn't willing to accept it as a permanent part of my life. It felt awkward, not knowing exactly what she wanted from me so we could end the conversation; it almost felt like she wanted me to make a pledge that I would never part from the chair. That was something I was unwilling to do, and when I left that day, I couldn't help but feel as though I disappointed her.

My PT sat down privately with my mom that same day and shared these thoughts with her after our conversation. She pleaded with her to stop pushing so hard for me to walk and to accept my fate. Life would go on; it would just be different. But if she continued to feed my determination to walk, I would be wasting away some of the best years of my life.

Although she understood my PT's concerns, my mom was more offended than anything. My mom knew me, the kind of person I was, and simply believed I would be able to overcome anything. Mom thought that even though the PT knew more about spinal cord injuries, she didn't know *me*, her son, as well as she did. She also knew she would never push me to the point of having me feel as though I had disappointed her. She only wanted to do as any parent would—support me while I gave it my all and live without regrets about not having done my best—just as she had all my life.

When we finally left the hospital, it was with grateful hearts. The doctors, nurses, and therapists had all done their part to put me on a path that would allow me to make my own way. I had gone from a helpless state to one I could manage. This gave me the freedom of choice, being free to create and determine what I would do with my life without the worry of wondering if I would be okay. I knew I still had a life left, but I had no idea where my future would lead.

KEEP LOOKING UP

During this time in my life, I spent a lot of time looking down, thinking things like, *As long as I don't fall ... As long as I don't make a misstep ... As long as I don't screw up ... I need to be really careful.* I'd watch every step because it was important to see my own feet moving.

When I had the opportunity to walk with the Lokomat and started getting used to the feeling of it, I was able to look up again. Don't get me wrong—every so often I'd check to see my feet moving along on the treadmill as the robotics velcroed to the outside of my legs did their job. I wasn't close to walking on my own, but I had these childlike moments when I felt like I was just walking outside.

And I'd look up.

I'd remind myself that I was upright and that I was experiencing a super cool moment.

The more I worked with the Lokomat, the easier it was to shift my focus away from the mechanics of walking. I started relearning how to move my arms along with the opposite foot. Then I started to check out the new scenery. The facility was just outside of a mall, so I'd see cars driving by and snowflakes making their way to the ground. I'd look to the left and to the right, seeing other people working out, posters on the walls, just anything and everything around me.

Where I live now, there are beautiful unobstructed views of the sunset along the horizon line. And every night I have a choice. I can stand outside staring at my feet, making sure I'm safe, or I can take the time to look up and see the incredible thing God is doing right in front of me.

It's so easy to focus on the pain and the stress of what you're going through at any given moment, but allow yourself a little time throughout your days to look up. If you can, go outside or look out a window. Take five minutes to journal about what you see when you choose to shift your focus, and reflect on how it makes you feel.

USE WHAT WORKS FOR YOU

There is a difference between having determination and being stubborn.

For me, determination was wanting to make all these people proud—whether it was my dad and Hollis, my mom who was there cheering me on, visitors, or later in the story, Elliot, Mike, or Parker. I was able to dig deep and keep going ... for them.

I've always felt like stubbornness was a negative thing. If you could ask someone who knows me well to describe my personality, I don't think "Brock is stubborn" would make it into the conversation. I consider myself much more of a people-pleaser. I try to keep an open mind and listen to what others have to say, even to the point where I try to see things from their perspective.

I know it wasn't intentional, but I think I did naturally move between determination and stubbornness depending on the version of myself that was most beneficial for the situation. I'd start my mornings full of determination and then peak out. My determined mindset would taper off as I started feeling more exhausted and dragged down. Stubbornness showed up for me when I felt like I wanted to prove the naysayers wrong. I could hear their words in my mind. Things like, "You have a one-percent chance of walking again." "This wheelchair is a permanent part of you now." "You can't do this." "You shouldn't try to do that." And I'd answer them in my mind with, *Okay, I'm going to prove you wrong.*

You've read about the well-meaning (but unwanted) advice and warnings I received from my PT and other hospital staff members who had "been there and done that." With God's grace, I was able to continue to hear Him telling me that wasn't the case for me.

Let's look at what you can do when you are faced with excuses and comments that have the potential to hold you back or keep you from looking up. Grab your journal.

BROCK'S RULES FOR EVALUATING AND OVERCOMING EXCUSES

1. **Explain the "why" of your goal.** Sometimes it's just as simple as asking yourself how important your goal is to you. For example, maybe you're thinking about getting a master's degree. You may have thoughts like, *This will give me a bump up for my career.* For me, getting my master's was partially to show myself I could do it. But my main motivator wasn't getting another diploma or better pay. My goal with a master's degree was to establish the credentials I needed to be a public speaker, which in turn boosted my confidence.

- Take a moment to journal about that one big goal that has been on your mind.
    - Why do you want to achieve it?
    - For whom are you determined to achieve it?
    - How do you visualize your life after achieving it?

2. **Get clear on the self-talk that motivates you the best.** There were quite a few times in the gym when I was talking to myself out loud to help push myself to keep going. I'd get to the point where my body would tell me, *I can't keep going!* And I'd come right back with, *You will keep going!* And then I'd lie to myself, *You only have to take one more step, then you're done.* Once that step happened, I'd say it again.
    - Choose the kind of voice you want in your head to help you keep moving forward.
        - Is it more stubborn or determined? Why?
        - How will you express yourself *to* yourself?
            - Will you write yourself notes, talk in your head or out loud, give yourself voice notes, or some other way?

3. **Practice the art of a "temporary yes."** Even though I knew I didn't want my wheelchair to be a permanent part of my life, I accepted that it was going to be a temporary part as I continued to heal. Knowing this, I had to say yes to spending time learning how to use my wheelchair in situations where, for example, an elevator might not be available or a building entrance might have a high

threshold with no ramp. That temporary yes didn't mean I was abandoning my goal of walking and not having to use a wheelchair, but it acknowledged that my current situation required some slight detours on the path to my ultimate goal. But the destination never changed.

- Can you identify situations in your life where a "temporary yes" might be beneficial?
- How do you balance acknowledging your current situation with maintaining focus on your ultimate goals?
- In what ways can accepting a temporary solution be a strategic step toward achieving your long-term objective?

4. **Start with a small, obtainable goal.** Instead of starting a new midlevel manager job and saying you'll be the CEO of the company within a year, start with something that feels more attainable in the near future and can help you see that you've moved the needle in the ultimate direction you want to go.
    - Write down your one big long-term goal.
    - Then work backward, identifying milestones between where you are now and where you want to be.
        - What is one thing you can do each day, week, or month to move yourself forward?
        - How can you acknowledge or even celebrate these milestones?
        - Whom can you call on to support, encourage, or even challenge you to stay on track?

5. **Listen. Then make a decision based on who you are and how you feel.** It breaks my heart to think of all the people who might have listened to "experts" who had told them they *couldn't* or *shouldn't* try something, and because they valued other people's opinions, they just stopped trying altogether. If you keep hearing that little voice inside telling you to go after your next degree, start a business, or whatever it may be, it's okay to listen to people as they share their opinions. But you can interpret what they're saying in the same way as when an adult told you as a child to put on a warm coat when it was cold outside. They're probably well-meaning, just trying to protect you in their own way. And when you can see their words as a suggestion rather than a command, you can make the final decision for yourself.

   * Create a phrase you can use when someone shares an opinion about why you should stop going after your goal.

CHAPTER 5

FRUSTRATION AND FORGIVENESS

Shortly after returning home, I learned that a court date had been set for the man who ran the stop sign on Christmas Eve. What had become of that man was far from my mind through everything that I was dealing with, so receiving the court notice was a jarring reminder of the accident.

It was painful to realize that I had been trapped in a hospital for the entire five months leading up to the actual court appearance. I hadn't really considered what punishment there might be for the driver, but I knew it would be insignificant compared to what my family and Hollis's family had suffered.

The man voluntarily gave up his license after the accident, but it wouldn't be until the court hearing that his actual punishment would be decided. I was completely unaware of what might actually happen, but I thought it must be similar to what a drunk driver would face after costing others their lives.

In the short time I had to consider it, I couldn't believe the selfishness and recklessness of this ninety-two-year-old driver. It was sobering to think of how long he might have been putting people's lives at risk so he could just continue driving.

THE TRIAL

On the day of the trial, my family members and I sat with the prosecuting attorney before going into the courtroom. He let us know that we would have the opportunity to speak if we so desired. I knew I wouldn't enjoy speaking, but that feeling was overcome by the reality that I simply couldn't turn down the only opportunity I would have to share with the driver how I felt about what had happened.

The prosecutor warned us not to expect much. The judge was limited with what he could hand down in punishment due to the man's age. It was hard for me to understand how someone could be too old for jail but not for driving. It seemed to me the implication was that once you passed a certain age, you were no longer responsible for carelessness.

In the courtroom, the defense attorney opened by pointing to the unfortunate reality that these things happen. He said that each of us had most likely accidentally run a stop sign, but in this case, the simple mistake had devastating consequences. He went on to explain that all the apologies in the world wouldn't change what happened and that he hoped we could finish the session quickly and get everyone "back to our lives."

Wouldn't that be nice? However, unfortunately for our family and Hollis's, our lives were in shambles. Our loved ones could not just *get back to their lives.* It angered me to see how the defense attorney tried to make a life-shattering event sound like it was as easy to get over as a glass of spilled milk.

After the brief opening, the judge allowed the victims' families to speak. As members of my family spoke, I could hear an obnoxious whisper coming from somewhere behind me and across the aisle. He was related to the man who ran the stop sign—maybe his adult son or son-in-law. But he was huffing and puffing comments about how unfair this whole thing was, like a disgruntled child. His comments were just loud enough to hear over the crying that came from both sides of the aisle.

As my aunt talked about how the state was asked to move the elderly man's mailbox across the street so he didn't have to cross it to get his mail, someone from the defendant's side of the courtroom shouted, "That's a lie!"

My aunt turned to face him and said, "That is a fact."

Immediately the judge commanded her to address the court only. For some reason, the defendant's family's shouting was ignored.

My aunt continued to explain that the defendant's family was concerned about his ability to cross the road to get his mail, presumably because his vision had grown so poor. Yet he still drove.

She also said his punishment should include being required to provide some community service, as he still mowed his own lawn and surely insisted on doing many things for himself. She suggested the judge not recuse him from being required to do something for someone else after causing such a tragic accident.

As our family continued to share their victim statements, I kept trying to ignore the obnoxious whispers from that same man behind us. Then I had my chance to address the court. I rolled my wheelchair down the aisle, turned to face the judge, and spoke from my heart:

"I can't begin to explain the pain I've felt over the last few months. I've never dealt with anything like this in my twenty-three years of living, and I can't imagine what my life will be like now. I can't imagine living without my dad and Wauseon living without an angel like Hollis. As if that wasn't enough, I have to live every day in this chair. I know an apology won't change any of that, but neither will my forgiveness.

"But despite all of that, I want you to know, I do forgive you. Regardless of circumstances or excuses, I forgive you for having caused that accident. I don't know how, but I know my family will find a way to get through this. Although the burden is too much already, I have realized that forgiving you for what has happened is the only sure way to help ease that burden for me, at this moment. Even though you haven't asked for forgiveness, I would like to think in your heart you have asked for it in some way.

"An apology won't change any of what happened, and it may not mean anything to some people, but for me, it means something. It means everything to me here and now. I wouldn't ask for admittance of guilt or any acceptance of fault, but simply you stating you are sorry for this event. I have a million unanswered questions, but to have you say you wish this had never happened, as I have, would mean something to me."

I rolled my chair back up the aisle, positioning myself in the row next to my mom. I bowed my head to wipe my tears and pray as the trial continued. The judge turned to the defense to give them a chance to speak. The attorney turned toward the elderly man, and then he stood.

"My client declines to speak at this time."

It seemed as though I had just been slapped in the face. I was shocked. I couldn't believe that someone involved in such a tragic accident had absolutely *nothing* to say, in his one opportunity to speak to the victims of his mistake.

The judge continued, telling us one side would think his sentence is light, while the other would consider it harsh. He listed fines that would need to be paid by the defendant, around $1,000 in total.

The judge then said the defendant would serve two three-month terms of house arrest for each victim who passed away.

Again, I heard the obnoxious voice behind me, "That's so stupid ... Just stupid."

I fought the urge to turn around, infuriated that I had just spent three-and-a-half months incarcerated in a hospital and would be in a wheelchair for much longer than the six months he would be in his home.

After the judge had finished, I was more than ready to just go home. I was disappointed, frustrated, and discouraged by everything that happened that day. But as I turned to leave, a group of women approached me from the other side of the aisle.

Tears soaked their faces as they expressed to me how sorry they were. I could only assume they were daughters and granddaughters of the man who had hit us. They were unable to say much, weeping as they spoke, but simply told us they were sorry. It was the only sign of remorse I saw that day, and it was a welcome one.

I wanted to see that someone cared about what happened, instead of thinking that it was fine for the man who hit us to go on with life as usual. It still hurt to know he wouldn't even speak given the chance.

Did he believe he was better than anyone else and that he could shatter the lives of a family as if nothing had happened? Or was he sorry for what he had done?

I later heard from a couple of people following the trial that he was very remorseful for what had happened and that he used to be a pastor. It made it even more confusing as to why he wouldn't speak that day.

It was less than a year after the trial that the man passed away. I only saw him twice in his life—the night of the accident and the day in court. Hearing about his passing after being blessed with over ninety years of life made me consider my own life. I thought about things I would not want to leave unsaid and the kind of legacy I would want to leave behind.

Blake

Our dad was a very laid-back, happy, and easygoing kind of guy. I remember playing cards with him on the night of the accident, and when I tried to steal some of his poker chips, he leaned back as he pushed some over to me, saying, "Here, you can have 'em. Take 'em. Go ahead."

I think his positive outlook on life is a legacy that he passed on to all three of us, for sure.

I heard the quote, "To forgive is to set a prisoner free and discover that the prisoner was you."[1] If you dwell on those negative things, it's really doing more harm than good. I think that's where we're fortunate, to have been brought up the way we were, and hopefully, we carry ourselves the right way.

When we were growing up, our dad, David, nearly always had a contagious, jovial attitude. He had a way of lifting our spirits and motivating us to be excited about nearly anything.

NOT EASY, BUT NECESSARY

Moving home solidified the reality that I wasn't going to wake up from the nightmare and go back to the way things were before the accident, but at the same time, it had whisperings of a new start. It was the culmination of my surgeries, healing, and struggling through physical therapy to be able to leave the hospital. It represented the turning of a page with new hope for what came next. Revisiting the accident by having to face the trial so quickly was definitely an extra page I didn't see coming.

For me, part of moving on from the accident was to offer my forgiveness without being asked. I don't know how many times in my life an offer of forgiveness without receiving an apology in return happened. But I pushed myself into the old man's shoes and worked to convince myself through the pain that this person didn't get into his car that night for the sole purpose of hurting us.

Don't get me wrong—it was another internal battle over time. It wasn't one of those clear-cut turning points where I said I forgave him and then never thought about him again. It was a way for me to understand how I wanted to live my life going forward.

I couldn't live feeling bitter about what happened all day every day. I remember when I was still in the hospital, I would ask myself, *Why am I here?* And my brain played along with a very logical response, *Because a man ran a stop sign.* It was just that simple.

For the most part, after that day, a little bit of the weight had lifted. And a little more as the days continued. Sometimes it would come in waves. I would be angry on the hard days. More than a statement to the judge or the man, I think my victim statement was speaking to God. I wanted to be the kind of man who could forgive and move forward. And no matter how much I would waver or falter over my feelings, He could help me with it. That statement was a commitment to myself and to Him. This is what my faith tells me to do, and this is what I plan to do in my own imperfect, human way.

CHAPTER 6

RECLAIMING MY LIFE

That fall, I was determined to reclaim as much of a sense of normalcy in my life as I could. After three and a half months in a hospital, arriving home and putting the trial behind me was the perfect transition point for me to begin to focus on the future. And I decided to begin by finishing my coursework at Ohio State. It would take just over two months to get the final fifteen credits and my degree in economics. I looked forward to the challenge of going back to school and finishing what I had started.

It was fairly easy to find physical therapy at Ohio State in a location not far from where I had my classes. The difficult part for me was going back to a place where few people knew what had happened to me. I worried that I would have to explain what happened to these new therapists, which would be fine, but I hated the idea of them feeling sorry for me. Anytime I felt this way, I tried to remind myself of how fortunate I was to have people who cared enough to ask.

As I prepared to attend my first day of classes, I also grew concerned about talking to the new people I would meet. After my injury, I realized one of the first things people would notice when meeting me was my wheelchair. For me, it seemed easier to address my situation in my own way, rather than avoid it or wait for someone else to bring it up.

Most people would understand that whatever my story was, it wasn't going to make for a positive icebreaker. At the same time, it was something that changed the way I lived in a major way, despite my not having chosen it.

In one particular instance, I was pleasantly surprised by a fellow student who began a conversation with me before class.

The conversation started out completely normal, then took a sudden twist. He began by letting me know that I didn't have to talk about it but he just had to ask as he pointed in the general direction of my wheelchair toward the back of my legs.

Here it comes, I thought to myself.

But as he continued, I realized his question had nothing to do with my situation and everything to do with the bright maize University of Michigan letter *M* sticker at the back of my wheelchair. He smiled as he admitted that the symbol was pretty rare at The Ohio State University.

I laughed under my breath, shaking my head.

I went on to share my story, including how my brother ended up going to Michigan. It was refreshing to hear that he thought my story was quite extraordinary and he never expected to hear anything like it when he decided to ask about a simple sticker. We continued to chat, and he admitted that he might hate "that team up north" a *little* less after our conversation.

BACK TO SCHOOL

I struggled to get back into a routine at OSU. I hadn't been studying books or writing papers for over a year. Classes weren't exceedingly difficult, but it was much harder for me to sit in place at a desk for any period of time. Usually, my mind would drift off to think about how I could be exercising, and sometimes that led me to try to move my legs right under the desk. When my thoughts of walking again overcame my thoughts on business strategies, I would give in and go to the gym.

Ohio State has an incredible facility known as the RPAC (Recreation and Physical Activity Center) where students can go work out. I wasn't sure what I could do there, but I found a program that gave me someone to help me through a workout regimen. It was a lot of work to even get in a position to work out my legs, but with the help of a volunteer, I was able to burn some of the energy that had built up.

My last quarter of school went by quickly, and before I knew it, it was graduation day. I hated the fact that I couldn't walk up to get my degree, but I was able to go up on the stage to receive it myself, which was a blessing. Thousands of students graduated alongside me, and we were all reminiscing about what it took for us to get to that day.

It was bittersweet for me, considering everything I had been through. I also considered my future and where my life would lead next. I thought a lot about the patience I would need to persevere.

In the meantime, I was fortunate enough to meet the director of recreational sports, who offered me a job at the RPAC. I had a reasonable schedule and got a workout before or after a shift. On my off days, I would go back to physical therapy to try crawling, kneeling, or walking in the leg braces. We had started to walk in the parallel bars, but the process remained frustratingly painful to set up. I was improving on my four-point stance, but it seemed to be due to a stronger core and upper body rather than a renewed strength in my legs.

My PT was very supportive, giving me a challenge by having me try a three-point stance or try to stand in the braces with just one arm holding the bar. Working, workouts, and physical therapy were difficult enough, but there were other obstacles to deal with as well.

BACK BEHIND THE WHEEL

One major obstacle I still had to face was learning to drive without using my legs. It frustrated me to think about having my driving skills tested all over again. When I was sixteen, I went through classes and drove for hours with my permit before taking the driving test.

Before graduating high school, I obtained my pilot's license. At the age of twenty, I received a commercial driver's license to drive a tractor-trailer. The testing didn't bother me at all but rather that I had to show that I was a skilled, safe driver, despite the fact that our accident—my injury—was caused by someone who didn't pass those standards.

When I finally scheduled my first "test drive" utilizing hand controls rather than the standard pedals, I cast my frustrations aside and was simply looking forward to regaining more independence. When I met my instructor, I took the liberty of sharing with her some of my past skills and assured her that learning to drive with my hands would not be a problem.

I had been told previously that it was sometimes hard for people to become accustomed to the change, but the instructor was pleasantly agreeable to my opinion. She seemed reassured when I wasn't worried, and she welcomed me to climb into the driver's seat of the car whenever I was ready.

I placed my right foot on the floor of the car using my right hand to lift it. Then I pressed my fist into the seat and leaned my head forward to lift my butt over and into the seat. My mom came from the other side of the car to roll my wheelchair away, and she wished me good luck. As I pulled my other leg into the car, the instructor got into the passenger's seat.

She explained the push-pull control (pull to accelerate, push to brake), and I guessed that the spinner knob on the wheel was to make turns without going hand over hand.

At first, accelerating was clumsy at best. After shifting out of park, I felt a quick burst, followed by a sudden loss of power. I half smiled, slightly embarrassed, as I steered around the parking lot and tried to correct my initial miscalculation. I rested my arm fully on the armrest, and then I was finally able to gain more control for a nice, smooth acceleration. I eased the car to a stop at the end of the parking lot, waiting to enter the road leading around the nearby mall.

I was able to accelerate just fine to twenty-five miles per hour and turned my focus to the stop sign up ahead. As we approached, I could feel a twitching in my leg. I had to think for a moment and then pushed on the hand control to start slowing down. As I came to a stop, I realized how naturally my leg wanted to move to the brake pedal. I took a deep breath and kept my focus on the hand control.

My instructor was very encouraging during our trip and even offered some highway driving for an exit or two. Without hesitating, I used my turn signal to move over toward the on-ramp. Once again I was able to accelerate smoothly up to the speed limit, this time to merge in with traffic. It felt great to finally feel that sense of freedom, being able to drive again.

The trip was fairly short but well worth it. The instructor told me she was certain I wouldn't need a long, extensive training program and would be ready to test today if I could. I just needed to find the right time to take the test in Ohio.

Over the summer, I planned when I could start driving classes in September so that I could graduate in December. I also found an instructor and car to use for a driving test, which would definitely come in handy once I was back on my own in Columbus. Fortunately, the instructor had agreed that I wouldn't need a lengthy training process, but she offered the idea of practicing parallel parking just before the test and found an opening for me to finally get my license.

On my first try, I passed my driving test and got my license back. Luckily, a friend from home who owned a car dealership was able to make arrangements to help me overcome my next challenge—replacing my truck with a car equipped with hand controls.

MOVING FORWARD

Having my newly acquired freedom, I decided to work toward my graduate degree. I entered the School of Public Affairs at OSU, wanting to learn more about our government and, more importantly, nonprofits. I thought in the future I would be able to use the degree to help someone else who was going through a similar situation but didn't have a clue how to get started. I'd be better prepared for what I knew could be a bright future of helping others get through their struggles after I was through my own.

During that time, I began to get discouraged with physical therapy, especially as my increasing obligations weighed me down. I realized that given the small amount of progress I had made, it would be unrealistic to expect my energy and finances to last at the rate things had been going.

I felt torn between putting energy toward my degree or physical therapy. I was spending time in school, with friends, and doing so many other things that I had missed during my recovery. I had been praying to God for guidance, not sure if I was supposed to continue on this course or move on with my life and the things I had wanted to do before the accident.

While it seemed I had been waiting so long for an answer to many prayers, I still couldn't be sure how or when I would receive one. As I waited for my answer, I would drive home on the weekends from Columbus and every now and then make it up to Ann Arbor to see Elliot either before or after football practice. Most of the people within the practice area knew me and always greeted me at the front door. It was a great honor, and I felt as though I could always gain some encouragement from watching how hard the team worked.

GOING FOR IT

It was in October of 2009 that I decided to visit my brother once again at practice. As usual, I was greeted by strength coach Mike Barwis as I rolled into the football complex. He greeted me with his unmistakable raspy voice, asking if I was coming in to work out with him. I chuckled and told him I was dressed to work out if he really wanted to. Practice was about to start, so he told me to stop by before I left so he could run me through some things he thought might help.

It was hard to focus on the team's practice while thinking about what Mike might want to put me through. I worried Mike would realize how bad off I actually was and not want to work with me as adamantly as he had tried to for the last two years.

I recalled Elliott's warning: Mike wasn't someone to cut *anyone* slack. Maybe he would continue to push me no matter what, and it made me wonder if I would hit a breaking point. Other thoughts raced through my head: *If I'm willing to do what most people don't even consider (whether because it's not realistic or too difficult), would I get the chance to accomplish what most people never achieve?*

My anticipation made the practice go by quickly, and I started to make my way toward the weight room as players went to the locker room. I knew I was ready for a change in my routine and thought this could be the answer I had been waiting for. As great as the opportunity seemed, it was also a massive challenge, one that many people wouldn't accept given there was only *a chance* that progress could be made.

Whether the chance was one percent or fifty percent, it would be impossible to know what the result would be. I knew I would have to make a decision, whether to give up or give 100 percent of my time and effort into a workout built for *an athlete*. Having been through so much, I knew I was ready to be treated as a strong person again. I had been treated like I was weak for too long, and I knew I was ready to test myself.

As I rolled into the weight room, Mike was talking to a small group of five or six people in suits. I patiently waited behind them. Mike turned, somehow realizing I had snuck up on them, and glanced back at me. He then dismissed who I later found out were a group of NFL scouts, telling them he had to get to work, and shook each hand while saying goodbye.

Having a hop in his step, Mike came over to me, rubbing his hands together, asking if I was ready to get to work. I told him I was and couldn't wait to try something new. He reiterated to me, as he did before, that he had never worked with someone who had a spinal cord injury, but he still believed he could help me. Today, he said, he wanted to try a number of different exercises, to see what I could and couldn't do.

After the brief introduction, we went right over to one of the weight racks where players would squat, bench, and do most of the more popular lifts. Mike said he wanted to just have me stand in the rack, to see how my legs felt and handled it.

There was no question this was an ambitious exercise, especially as the first one of the day. Mike knelt in front of me, telling me to grab the sides of the rack to help myself up as he held and guided my knees. My knuckles turned white as I gripped as hard as I could, pulling myself up despite feeling the weight of my body sinking slowly. Mike pressed my knees, lifting me up, until I was standing straight, clutching the bar in front of me to keep from falling.

Mike asked what I felt in my legs. In honesty, I told him that there wasn't much I felt, except an uneasy feeling of unsteadiness around my waist. He told me to try to focus on whatever I could, to see if I felt more stable leaning back, forward, or wherever. I couldn't position myself in any way that was preferable to the other. As I sat back down, he didn't seem at all dissuaded from working with me.

Although I felt as if I should have had a breakthrough, Mike reassured me that he still had some ideas to help me along and had learned a lot from that exercise. It was a welcome surprise, having thought that without feeling, there wouldn't be any hope. Mike could tell my legs had changed color, from pasty white to dark blue. He pressed a finger lightly against my knee, watching the color white slowly turn blue as he removed it.

Mike wanted to see how much I could move my legs, so I tried to pull them up off the mat. My knee came off the mat, as my hips were able to pull them up, and he asked how that felt. I told him it was as though there was a huge weight surrounding my leg. That was about the extent of what I could do, although while I sat in the chair, I could kick my leg a little. Mike grabbed onto my right leg to help lift it up, then told me to try to keep it there. He slowly pulled down, making the weight feel much heavier, slowly straightening the leg as it dropped.

He told me these "eccentric" lifts would be very important to me as we went through my recovery process, giving me further confidence that I wasn't going through a trial run; *Mike was in for the long haul.*

Mike reintroduced me to his coordinator of strength and conditioning, Parker Whiteman, during our workout. I had met him before but hadn't realized that someday I would be there working out with him. Mike told me he thought Parker would be an important part of my recovery as well, knowing he wouldn't be able to help me himself for long enough stretches. Parker's shaved head made him stand out, along with his deep voice and polite demeanor. He greeted my mom with a hug and genuinely wanted to know how everything was going.

As we talked, Mike and Parker helped lift me over onto a balance ball, asking me to simply try to sit on my own. It wasn't too long ago that it was a challenge for me to simply sit on a solid surface without back support. They gradually let go of my shoulders, as I tilted back and forth between them, and eventually settled for ten seconds before falling and reaching for an arm. Although I couldn't sit for more than twenty or thirty seconds on my own, I told them I could definitely feel my abs burning. I knew building on that would be crucial if I was going to be able to stand on my own one day.

We went through about a dozen more workouts that day, with mixed results, but mostly what some would describe as failure.

Elliott

I had gone through a full football season at Michigan and was going into spring football practice about a year after the accident. Brock was in his wheelchair with my mom and Blake. At that time, Brock was moving his legs a little. We'd see a foot move and go nuts, yelling, "Oh my gosh, you just kicked your leg!" And then he'd try the other one.

I remember going through the weight room when I heard Mike call Brock over. He and my mom were there to watch a spring practice. I was supposed to be dialed in on the practice that was about to start, but I couldn't help overhearing Mike saying, "If you want to walk again, we've got to start with your core. You have to have a firm core to be able to pull those legs up to your stomach and then walk heel to toe. I don't know how to make somebody walk again, but I know the human body, and I know how to make someone a peak athlete. If you want to figure this out together and you're willing to put in the work, I think I can make you walk again."

I fully trusted Mike. I had been with him for a year. It didn't take long after meeting him for me to realize that he might be the exact kind of mad scientist we needed to make things happen for Brock. Mike was never the kind of guy who just said, "We're going to work really hard, and you can't stop until you puke." He was much more thoughtful, always on the experimental side of things. He was consistently actively educating himself.

He'd do research, learn something new, and apply it. We'd be so broken down we couldn't even lift a finger in the air, but three weeks later, we'd be the strongest we'd been in our whole lives.

I knew he wasn't the kind of person to just take my brother who couldn't walk, throw him around, and see if he could make something happen. I knew how working with him that first year had changed my body. As much as we hated his workouts, we absolutely loved him and would run through a wall for him.

I knew my brother would be in good hands with Mike. I knew it was really the only path, but it wasn't going to be easy to watch.

A NEW BEGINNING

To me, the entire day was just setting the starting line. Any doubts I had were gone by the time I left. I talked to Mike one-on-one in his office before he left that day. He told me he would never want to give me the idea that he was going to "fix me," but rather he wanted to give me the assistance, tools, and direction for me to overcome my injury.

He said he was limited in his knowledge but believed that somehow God had a plan for him to use his gifts to help me in my journey. He believed this was the way to show God we believed. We would leave the healing up to Him while we did all we could here on earth.

For me, that statement confirmed that I was in the right place. He explained that he could see the determination in my eyes—similar to what he saw in great athletes—that I would do whatever it took to walk again. That made him believe that between me and God, we would get it done.

He told me about his time in medical school and the way he developed his method of training athletes. He told me about Wolff's Law: the body will conform and adapt to the directions and stresses it is habitually exposed to. And he believed that simple statement would apply to me as much as any other person. I couldn't say I understood everything he explained to me, but I knew he understood it, which was all I needed.

I took the weekend to prepare for my first "official" workout on Monday. I would arrive at the football complex at nine o'clock, just after the players finished their lift. Mike told me I could take a break for lunch at eleven, as more players would be lifting, then start another workout at noon. I knew it wouldn't be easy.

Usually, I was ready for a nap after a couple of hours of physical therapy, so it would be interesting to see how it would go once I was put through their full workout. I tried to rest as much as possible over the weekend, but I also tried to stretch and eat well. I knew if I was going to make it through the first week of workouts, I had to do all I could to give myself a good start.

I was greeted by the lady at the front desk window inside the football facility when I arrived. It felt good to be welcomed as a part of the family. She told me I didn't have to sign in; I could go right on in as always. As I went through the door, passing through the hallway decorated with the photos of previous Michigan teams, I felt as though I would be able to achieve something great as well.

I turned to my right, toward the weight room, and read the words above the door: *Through these doors walk the hardest working athletes in the world.* I could have felt a lot of pressure because of that, but instead, I felt an overwhelming sense of confidence. I knew I had an opportunity, one that no other person in the world had received in the same way, and I fully believed I was capable of making the most of it.

I could hear Mike yelling inside the weight room even over the loud music, the grunting players, and the noise of weights being thrown around. He took long strides, walking back and forth past the weight racks. He'd stop at a rack as a player was about to lift, squatting down with his hands on his knees, as he'd yell to pump up the player before his lift. As the bar bounced off the ground following a lift, Mike would jump up to slap the player on the chest for having accomplished his goal. I knew I would have a great motivator pushing me toward my goal, and I couldn't wait to get started.

As soon as the team broke the huddle following the lifting session, Mike came over to get started with me. As the players left, they came up to shake my hand and say hello. Some of them smiled, offering their own warnings about agreeing to work with Mike. Mike assured me that I shouldn't be anxious about that. Most of it was true about how hard he would push, but it was better not to worry.

He told me he had a great idea as we went over to the same rack we had used the week before. Mike grabbed two thin ropes from the top of the rack, unraveling them from around two arms with pulleys on the end. One end of the rope was attached to a pulley on the bottom of the rack. Mike had me put a belt around my chest and under my arms, and he attached the other end of each rope to the belt.

Mike stepped on a switch that ran along the bottom sides of the rack, and a hiss of air ran into a tank, causing the ropes to start pulling me up. A set of digital numbers ran up, showing the pounds of resistance (or in my case, *assistance*) going through the machine. The belt started to rise up as the numbers reached seventy, then eighty pounds. As it rose over one hundred, I started to help and raise myself into an upright position. It seemed easier to stand, although more uncomfortable, with the harness.

Mike wanted me to try and squat down as well as I could, as he knelt down to guide my knees. They were already wobbling as I started to try and squat. Mike reached out to help keep them in place. I slowly eased my way down to having some bend in my knee and then tried to pull myself up. Mike thought it was great and that even if I wasn't feeling much, it would help the circulation and would have my nerves sending signals.

We continued with nine more repetitions, and sweat began dripping down my face. Each rep, unlike any squats I had done before, took sixty to ninety seconds to complete. The majority of the time was spent slowly watching my knees bend and my butt sitting back toward the bench behind me. This became an aerobic workout, leaving me out of breath, which was atypical to squatting before my injury. After the set, I felt as though I had just finished ten minutes of sprinting!

I sat back down when we finished the reps, feeling as much of a workout as I had ever felt in the last two years. I still felt like my arms were doing more work than my legs, but again, there was an obvious change in the color of my legs. Mike wanted to do two more sets of the workout after a short break, too short for me to catch my breath. Even though it only got harder as we went on, I was thrilled to be able to get to do something new. Getting the chance to see my legs in new positions and uniquely moving was a bonus as well. This gave me hope that I could continue to see new developments each week, or even each *day*, bearing in mind this was just the first week with Mike.

I returned every day that week and went all in on various other trial workouts. Mike told me he was as convinced as ever that I would walk, but the real work would start the following week. I considered how difficult the week had been and couldn't imagine how things could be *harder.* Mike had already pushed me to my limits—I would stop exercising once I could no longer move my legs.

How much more could I do?

The following week I would discover what else I had left after I couldn't do any more.

Many of our workouts were unconventional. Here I wore Mike's climbing harness to allow the air weight system to assist me in squatting. Parker was often my spotter, and Elliott would drop in to check on my progress.

Mike Barwis

The day I met Elliott and Brock, I remember thinking, *I got twenty-seven championship rings in about every sport you can imagine, and none of them matter.*

The human beings we come into contact with every day are what matters. Their lives matter. I could tell you about every kid I ever worked with, from elite athletes to people on the medical side. I could tell you about their families and their struggles. That's the only thing that's ever mattered to me.

From the time my kids were three years old, I've asked them, "What is fear?" and they've learned to respond with, "It's a liar." I believe that everything in life that you want is on the other side of your fears and inhibitions. If you allow them to hold you down or pull you away from what you were designed for, you're limiting your growth, and you're limiting the ripple effect that you can have on other people.

Deciding to work with Brock was simple. I cared deeply about Brock and his family, and they were asking for help. God gave us the opportunity to work together, and I'm not the kind of guy who could turn it down. I was trying to do the best I could to impact their lives positively.

Nobody cares how much you know until they know how much you care. The reality for me is that I love the people I work with, and they know it. So I can push them really hard, and it's okay with them.

I can be as tough as I need to be. When they leave, we hug. I tell them I love them. And they tell me they love me—it's everyone I work with, no matter what they're working on. I finish a workout with a 350-pound lineman, and we hug and exchange I-love-yous. He might have been in a trash can throwing up five minutes before that, and it's okay. I still love him.

But some days when they're just tired, you get to take your foot and put it in their butt. You have to make them move. *We're going to move forward. I'm not asking for your excuses. If you want to make progress, this is where we're going. I expect you to give me all you've got.*

If I can motivate you, and we love each other enough that you're willing to fight as hard as I'm asking you to fight, you'll have some success. If you're only fighting as hard as you're asking *yourself* to fight, it's going to be a struggle. It's not easy to push yourself that hard. You will always quit on yourself before you quit on others.

I show up every day because I'm fighting for them. They show up every day because they're fighting for me. And next thing you know, we've got a team. We can go a long way. That type of mentality is something that has to be produced when we're asking somebody to do the impossible.

> Somebody has to care enough to support them when they fall. When they do, we help them get back up. And when they hit the wall, that's when we let them know it's okay. "It's coming. I promise we're going to get there. Keep your head down, let's keep hammering. Don't give up. Here's where we're going."
>
> I've seen a lot of people who turn against God. "Why did you do this to me? What's wrong with me?" It's amazing when those people get back on their feet. I've had people tell me, "You're an angel." But I'm just a man. It's not me. God's the one healing you. I'm just a guy who works here, and I'm giving it the best shot I have to make my impact on your life. That's it.

CRAWLING ACROSS THE FLOOR

The real work started as soon as I rolled into the gym. We went directly to the squat rack, strapping the belt around my chest and hearing the air as it raised me up. The weight assistance was set at 190 pounds, which was a great portion of my body weight, and I used my hands to control the rest of the weight.

Since just standing in a frame wore me out, actually having to bear the weight with my arms and bent knees took a lot out of me. I could feel the sweat burning my eyes, and my legs felt even more like dead weight than before. My breathing was heavy and fast, making my throat dry. By the fifth rep,

I felt as though I was doing a chin-up, but we continued on until we reached ten.

Mike felt I could handle it okay, so he decided to drop the assistance to 185 pounds and told me to try using less arm strength as I lifted up—a very ambitious request considering the first set had worn me out already!

As we continued through each set, I had to continually have a new towel to dry off the sweat dripping down my face. While I wiped my brow, Mike would ask how the legs felt and give me directions for the next set. I was surprised by how much my responses seemed to affect the next set of workouts.

Mike would adjust the weight, how low I would squat, or the amount of time I would rest based on what I *thought* I could feel in my legs or abs. Rather than assuming I was just having wishful thoughts, hoping I was feeling something positive, he took my opinion as fact and based the workouts on those feelings.

Workouts became more and more difficult, with Mike pushing me further each time. Once we finished the first half of the workout, I felt completely drained. I tried to do some light stretching during the break, and Mike told me he was going to leave me to Parker as he trained some of the football players. I knew Parker would give me all I could handle as well, so I tried to get something to eat, but I didn't even have enough energy to chew and swallow.

Parker walked up and squatted down in front of me, "You better get your mind right. This set is going to get serious."

I took in a deep breath, sweat dripping as I exhaled. "I'll get there, just need a sec."

"You've put a lot in today, but you ain't finished yet," Parker told me. "I know you must be hurtin', but this is where you'll get the big payoff. You just gotta pay the price."

I nodded as I continued to try and catch my breath, trying not to think about how I was going to get through the second half of my workout.

I started the afternoon on the mat, unsure of what to expect. Parker said he wanted to get me moving around without my chair and asked me to get in a four-point stance on my hands and knees. I had tried to do some balancing in this position before, but Parker wanted me to start by trying to lift alternating hands up while I was kneeling.

It was a difficult warm-up to my next workout, which was crawling from one end of the mat to the other. I would place one hand in front of the other, then slowly try and pull one knee at a time a few inches forward. Each pull felt as though there was an anchor tied to my ankles. The mat was about ten yards long, and each yard seemed to take forever to complete, as the minutes passed by.

I knew each small step of my crawl would make a huge difference in my recovery, but it was so draining. It was discouraging to think about how I would ever find the strength to move past this challenge. I began to imagine all those days I was trapped in a hospital bed.

The time I was there, I felt a lot of pain, and I would have given anything to get rid of it. Now I was going after what I wanted, and I would have to get through the pain to get there. Each thought of never wanting to be back where I was kept me driven. I thought about not wanting to let anyone down, thinking about all the people who had come to visit and believed in me. I finally was within reach of the end of the mat.

As I rolled over to sit and rest after reaching the end of the mat, I was able to look back at the distance I covered. As short as it was, it seemed remarkable to me that I had been able to do it all without the chair, or any assistance for that matter. I realized it would just be a matter of time, with a consistent work ethic, that I would be crawling much farther.

It was inspiring to understand that I could finally see a path to improvement, and I recognized I wouldn't have to worry about how I would get to walking. It would be taken care of for me, just as learning to crawl had come.

There isn't only one person or event I can go back to and mention whenever someone asks me where my positive attitude or my determination to keep trying to walk again came from. I believe that between God's grace and the people He put in my life, I had an incredible foundation to build from when faced with adversity.

When I look back at this time in my life, it still amazes me that Mike dismissed NFL scouts (the men in suits) to come help me. The way that he and Parker didn't seem fazed by what I couldn't do and their laser focus on the potential of what I could do in the future made such a difference.

BROCK'S RULES FOR LIVING WITHOUT LIMITS

1. **Forget about who's watching or what they think.** Crawling across the floor made me decisively forget about how it might look to people who had no idea why I was doing what I was doing. It was fairly obvious from the onset that Schembechler Hall was full of visitors—sometimes even reporters taking pictures. I had moments when I'd think about people looking at me wondering, *What the heck is going on in there?* But then I had to remind myself why I was there. And those people began fading more and more into the background as I focused on what I was doing and why it was important to me.

   - Journal about the one thing you'd be willing to crawl across the floor to achieve.
   - Create a list of things that *won't* happen if you choose to stay right where you are without moving forward.
     - Whose opinions are keeping you from staying focused on your goal?
     - What could you accomplish if you chose not to focus on what other people think or what they see when you're working toward your goal?
     - Write down one thing you can say to remind yourself to keep going when you feel self-conscious or vulnerable.

2. **Ask yourself:** ***What will happen if I don't do this?*** I never told myself I wouldn't be able to walk again. I knew I was going to drive, finish my degree, and get my master's degree too. And when I showed up for my first workout, I knew that there was no way I was going to quit. Let's do some reverse engineering for a moment:

   - Create a list of things that *won't* happen if you choose to stay right where you are without moving forward.
     - What are the things you'll regret the most by choosing not to do the thing?
     - What will never happen to you as a result?
     - How will this affect the people around you?
     - Who would miss out on what you have to offer?

CHAPTER 7

GRINDING TOWARD THE GOAL

Each new drill took me that much closer to my goal of walking the Wolverines onto the field. It was excruciating at times, but I kept reminding myself that no matter how long it would take on that day, it would still be *one less* squat, *one less* crawl, or *one less* sit-up I would have to do in training.

Even during the brief moments when I wanted to give up on a rep and felt like I couldn't complete an exercise, I had Parker and Mike yelling at me not to quit. They seemed to recognize those faltering moments before I did, convincing me not to give in to the pain and fatigue that inevitably came. Each little breakthrough made me believe the next time would be easier than the one prior. I couldn't figure out how long it would take. I just knew that with this team, I would get where I wanted to go.

Mom

I'll admit, there are a lot of things in life that I didn't know about and couldn't predict. But I knew for sure that Brock would walk again. There were people at the hospital who literally said that I was crazy. I didn't care what they said. I wouldn't let them take that hope away from me.

Mike Barwis just connected with Brock like an angel walking into the room. I remember Mike giving me a big hug and saying, "Shelly, I may be the only one besides Brock, but I'm with you. Brock will walk again. I believe you with all my heart." It was the biggest miracle ever to have someone like Mike agree with me and give us hope.

He had a determined personality like Brock. I remember him saying, "That wheelchair is so ugly, you cannot take it into Schembechler Hall (the training center). I don't care how you get in here, but you are not bringing it in here." He had to crawl from the front door to where all the football players were and then crawl back out after his workouts. I wanted to go get the wheelchair and help him, but Mike said, "Don't you dare."

By the end of the first week, Mike had asked me to bring in my KAFOs and my walker. The knee-ankle-foot orthosis braces were built with a pendulum-like part in the knee that would allow it to bend in a certain position and then lock once again in the straightened position.

I didn't know how much or how little Mike would expect of me that day, but I looked forward to executing the plan. The setup process was as frustrating and painful as always, but it was worth the trouble once I was standing up again. I gripped the walker, arching my shoulders back to stretch my hips as I pulled it closer to my body. I looked down at my feet to ensure they were where I wanted them, then back up to see where I was going.

Mike Barwis, myself, and Parker Whiteman became family as we all lived in the weight room in 2010. As usual they are supporting me so I am able to be upright, on my own two feet!

I was standing at one end of the weight room when Mike said he wanted to see how I walked. I was shocked as he stepped back to have a better view, leaving my side. I was accustomed to having someone right next to me, ready at a moment's notice to rescue me from falling. I started to walk, leaning far onto my right leg before pulling the left one forward. I leaned onto my left leg again and then struggled to pull the right one forward. I already felt as though I had a good workout after just ten or twenty feet.

Mike and Parker didn't have much to say as they observed me. Without directions on where to stop, I continued on toward the wall. About forty feet into my walk, they told me I could sit down and helped me into a chair. It was also very hard to rest in the chair with my outstretched legs in front of me, but I tried to catch my breath while I could.

After several more walking attempts, Mike told me he thought we could strengthen my legs enough to let the braces bend at the knee without locking in the straightened position. He wanted to use some other air machines to strengthen my quads, making them able to bend so I wouldn't have to lean so much during each step. I knew my quads were still weak, but I believed we could do it.

He also wanted to work on my hamstrings in the meantime. They hadn't moved or even twitched at all. I lay on my stomach as he massaged the back of my leg and held my shin with his other hand.

"Go ahead and try to pull your heel to your butt," Mike suggested.

I gave it my all, closing my eyes and trying to focus on that one task.

"Anything?" I asked him.

"Nothing yet, but let me try something," he told me as he noticeably tried to massage much deeper into my leg. "Feel that?"

"Not a thing. Is that all you got?" I asked, amused.

Mike chuckled and smiled. "I see how it is, guess I need to stop taking it easy on ya in more than just these massages!"

I nervously laughed. "Well, I don't know about that. On second thought, I might be feeling something ... "

Although I was joking around that day, it only took about a month for me to start feeling something. At first, it was just a tingle, and I wasn't completely sure it was real. But over the course of the second month, I knew I felt it.

Then Mike would have fun as I would plead with him to let up—he finally had accomplished what he was trying to do. His goal was not to make me hurt but to have that nerve and, more importantly, the muscle, react to the stretch his finger was forcing on the inside of my leg. It was a much-appreciated improvement and one more thing I could work on and build up during the various workouts.

It was incredibly hard to have my legs put to work in so many different ways. Just as one thing became tiring, the next new exercise would seem even harder. My energy was spent a little more quickly each day. But somehow, with Mike and Parker, I was able to push through the wall I would hit every day ... and the next wall ... and even the next. There seemed to be no challenge we couldn't overcome one way or the other.

When even the yells of encouragement from them weren't enough, someone else on the staff would come by to press me forward, whether it was someone from Mike's staff or one of the many Michigan players coming through to start their workout. It was an incredible atmosphere—everyone was pushing everyone else to give their best. As hard as it was, I knew there was no other place I would rather be, especially when it came to trying to walk again.

Each day Mike set the bar way beyond what I thought I could do. Whether crawling or walking, my distance would double, even if it took half the day to complete. I would fail and fail again, then we would continue to try innovative exercises, in unusual ways if need be, which was often the case. When I would try and fail to balance with just one leg on the ground, Mike would have me hold someone's arm for as short of a time as I could before failing. Then I would gradually ease my grip and continue to try to balance.

When I was tasked with doing leg presses on the equipment, my only help came from Parker, pushing on my knees, helping only as much as he thought I would need. He allowed me to struggle for longer than I would have liked, giving me even more time to push. I would feel my feet tingle, my legs burn, and my face drip with sweat as I struggled. My thoughts were blank as I stared straight ahead, trying not to think about how difficult the presses were. After the second set, tears were coming out of my eyes. I didn't know if it was from the sweat burning in them or if I was pushing so hard even my tear ducts were emptying!

It was the first time I knew I had given literally 100 percent. I had never felt so worn out after a workout in my life, and Parker could see it.

He congratulated me on a great day of workouts and encouraged me by predicting that I would see great progress over the weekend from all the work I had put in. I was excited for the progress, but at that moment, it was enough for me to be able to rest.

Each day I came back, there was no doubt in my mind that I would be able to do what was asked of me. There was a fine line between my coaches' encouragement and the threat of what would happen if I gave up. I constantly kept the alternative to my workouts in the back of my mind: if I gave up, I would remain exactly where I was. It would put even more work in front of me, or worse, I would lose hope of ever walking again. That was something I could not accept, no matter how hard the work was to get there.

During this period, I had a lot of time to think, not only between each workout but while I commuted back and forth. At times it was a blessing; other times it was a curse. The true blessing was when I would dream of my increasingly brighter future and hope for further healing.

EYES ON THE PRIZE

A couple of months into these workouts with Mike, I remember Paker unexpectedly approaching me during what was my lunch break and his time with the student athletes' scheduled workouts. He said Coach wanted to see me, which was odd since I had just seen Coach Barwis that morning.

"Why does Mike want to see me again?" I asked.

"Not *that* coach, *the* coach, Coach Rod. Up in his office. Now," he retorted back with a serious tone I was unfamiliar with.

Of course, I immediately thought I had broken a rule or was in trouble for some other reason.

I started thinking about losing my scholarship, but I quickly remembered I didn't have one! I thought I might have to do extra workouts as punishment, but I didn't think that was possible since there were times they turned the lights off as I finished.

"Why do you think he wants to see me?" I finally asked as we made our way up the elevator to his office that overlooked the indoor football practice field.

"Probably just wanting to see how you're progressing. Anyone's guess."

After Parker knocked and we entered the office, Coach Rodriguez sprang up from his chair and smiled at us. He moved some chairs around to make room for my wheelchair by his desk and shook my hand. He asked how we were doing and how I was feeling. He asked Parker what kinds of workouts they were trying on me over the last couple of weeks. He was genuinely excited about the great strides we had made, and Parker went into detail about what we expected to do to get to the next step.

Coach Rodriguez leaned back in his chair and told me how proud he was at how well I'd taken on each challenge Mike and Parker had thrown at me. He said he had known from the day we met there was something special about me. Every day I went out to prove it, and with that, he wanted to offer me the opportunity he had mentioned that very first day we met.

"I want to give you a challenge—a tremendous opportunity—to lead us out onto that field for our opening game this fall. In about 200 days, you won't need the wheelchair to walk anymore. I'm certain of that. As long as you keep giving 100 percent every day, you can be right there with us when we take the field. I'd also like to share this with the team if you're willing. Until now, there have been rumors that walking with us is why you're here, but I want to make that vision a reality that the whole team is a part of."

I didn't know how to respond other than to say, "Yes."

That was absolutely what I wanted to do, and despite knowing how hard it still was to walk with leg braces and a walker or crutches, I knew I wanted to join my brother and lead his team on the field.

I knew it was a special moment, but I really didn't comprehend how special it was at the moment. Shortly after I left the office, I realized the immense pressure (which Parker "*kindly*" took the time to remind me of). Not only the team, but everyone would be aware of the expectations we had set—including more than 110,000 people in attendance that day! He reassured me that he and Mike would be right there with me along the way, and we would get me to where I needed to succeed in what so many thought to be impossible.

After Coach Rodriguez officially asked me to lead the team, I felt a new sense of responsibility for my workouts. Not only that, I started to realize how much pressure would be on me the day of the game. It was going to take extreme physical and mental preparation that spring if I was going to accomplish my goal in September.

I knew I would have to set up a game plan, but I had never known anyone who had done anything like what we were doing, let alone be crazy enough to set a timeline for it. I knew Mike would be the only person I could trust to dream up a plan and help me figure out what the road map to our goal would look like.

Then again, there weren't any great accomplishments I could think of where the person was given exact instructions on how to do it. Whether it was going to the moon, inventing the light bulb, or setting a new world record, they all required some level of blind faith.

The people who accomplished these feats had to believe they could do it without having any evidence that it was possible. Even if they had a guideline or used someone else's plan, it was impossible to know if it would work for them.

I also hadn't heard of anyone making progress the way I did with Mike during the last few months or had even tried the things we were trying. This gave me faith, knowing that I had already done what many thought to be impossible and that if we continued to do what few, if any, were willing to do, we would accomplish what few, if any, had ever accomplished.

Our workouts continued on a similar path, but there was even less rest time, which resulted in what seemed like longer days. I worked out five days a week, as well as some Saturdays. Many of these days, my legs felt like they couldn't do anything. We always found a way to get something moving and focus on it during the days I felt like my legs were weakest. It seemed to send a clear message to my legs that they had to do the work, regardless of how they felt. Every day I had to convince myself that those legs were still mine to command and they wouldn't be able to quit on me because of the injury.

As time grew closer, I was thrilled to hear ESPN's *E:60* wanted to do a follow-up story on our family. They had done a story on Elliott a year before. I was quoted at a football game during that episode, saying I hoped I would get to walk onto that field with my brother one day. I had no way of knowing that somehow I would begin to walk, let alone be asked to come onto the field before a game.

They wanted to show some of my workouts and be there for my big moment. Around that same time, a producer from the Big Ten Network also approached me about a story. They wanted to do a feature that was an in-depth look at the workouts I was doing with Mike and follow me the day of the game. It gave me a whole new sense of faith, seeing such big companies putting money behind showing our story. It thrilled me to know that even more people would be able to share in my big moment and share in the hope I was given.

I talked to Mike about what I should wear for the day of the game. I had considered wearing an Adidas Michigan shirt that read "Impossible is Nothing." I wore the shirt to workouts often and thought the saying fit perfectly.

Mike had other ideas. "You should make your own shirt. You have a chance to share a message with a lot of people, an opportunity almost no one gets. So you need to sit down and think about what you want that message to be. If you still decide to go with another shirt, that's your choice. But I say, make your own."

Parker agreed, knowing it was a rare opportunity.

I sat down that night to consider what my message would be. I thought about the past three years and what had kept me motivated. The first thing that came to mind was the initial one-percent chance I had been given.

I constantly thought, *There's a chance.* To me, the number didn't matter in itself, just that it wasn't zero percent. I had thought it cruel at the time for the doctor to give me such little hope. But as I thought about the message, I realized the surgeon *had* given me hope. I was blessed that I was given something, albeit a challenge, that I could strive for.

I also knew I would want to honor the memory of my dad and Hollis on the shirt. It felt like they helped me get up and make the most of every morning I was on earth. I knew my message would share with the huge crowd the kind of people they were. I also knew how big of a role God had played in how everything came together. I wanted to include my favorite verse during this time as well, words spoken by Jesus to a father who was asking for help for his son: *Everything is possible for one who believes* (Mark 9:23).

I felt compelled to come up with my own quote, and this verse from Mark gave me inspiration. I ended up with this: *Never settle for what others tell you is possible. Strive for the impossible.*

It was short and simple, but it was exactly what I did every single day. Even though many people had expressed how out of reach they thought my goals were, I knew my best life would come from achieving my huge goals—goals that most people would think were crazy. I had hoped sharing this simple thought would encourage others to go after whatever their dreams were.

I went to a website and created my design. Using a typewriter-style font, I put "Glory to God" at the top of the T-shirt's front, above a large "1%." On the back, I had "Mealer" across the top. Under that was my quote, then "Mark 9:23," and finally, "For David and Hollis." I was proud of the simple design, using a dark-blue-and-yellow color scheme, similar to the maize and blue of Michigan. It was clear to me that this was the shirt I wanted to wear. I purchased a couple dozen to share with family and friends the day of the game.

FALLING DOWN

Near the end of August, just two weeks before the game, I was still trying to walk with one cane and even no canes. I was determined to keep improving. Parker and Mike constantly reminded me that the walk onto the field wasn't my ultimate goal, so we had to continue to progress as much as we could each day we had. They started to push me past the ten-yard mark, shooting for fifteen or even twenty. Some tries would only get me two or three yards; for others, I would pass the ten-yard mark.

It motivated me to think we weren't just settling for good enough, especially given the huge event we had planned that was just over a week away.

At the time, it was a great try if I was able to pass the five-yard mark with one cane, and this was at the end of a solid workout. Despite my legs being drained after three or four attempts, I wanted to try making it over the goal line from the ten-yard line before calling it a day. Parker and Mike were only a few yards away after helping me get to a standing position. As I stood, I ran through everything I had to do over the next ten yards in my head.

After going through each step in my head, I started out with my right foot, paused briefly, and then brought my left foot up just enough to match my right toe. I continued this process through the five-yard line with Mike and Parker cheering me on with each step.

As I approached the goal line, I could feel my body sinking. I always kept my eyes on my feet as I stepped, so I immediately could tell it was my right knee that was giving out. I strained as much as I could to keep from falling, but I simply didn't have the strength left. It was clear that Mike and Parker fully believed I could make it, as they jumped under me at the last possible moment before I fell. This fall was a lot more awkward than the usual ones because I tried so hard to avoid the fall. Mike and Parker knew it was close, but they wanted to see how my ankle was after that particular fall.

I wasn't sure why, but I started to untie my shoe and take the strap off my ankle brace. My sock was soaked from sweat. My legs were finally sweating again and eventually even my feet. I commented that my feet were sweating again as I removed my sock. Underneath, we saw my entire ankle was a shade of blue.

"That looks like it really hurts," I told them.

Mike and Parker laughed at the comment, both nodding in agreement. Mike carefully rotated my ankle into a few positions, holding my leg in the air as he looked it over.

"Doesn't seem to be broken, but you're fine either way. If you don't feel it, might as well just walk it off!"

They each grabbed an arm, lifting me back up onto my feet.

"Still feels fine, or at least lacks any sensation of pain," I thought out loud.

Parker handed me my other cane as they each slowly released my arms. I felt fine walking, so Parker told me we could call it a day. As much as I had laughed it off, inside I breathed a deep sigh of relief knowing the fall wouldn't impede my walk at the season opener.

GETTING BACK UP

In the week leading up to the opening game, I was amazed at all the moments I experienced. As I worked out, the ESPN *College GameDay* bus showed up outside Schembechler Hall to interview the coaches and players. As I was walking on the indoor practice field, the Wolverines' star quarterback, Denard "Shoelace" Robinson, was being interviewed by ESPN reporter Erin Andrews.

It was incredible to be so close to something most people would give anything to see. I tried to continue with my workout on the indoor field, walking with one cane to the ten-yard line and back. At the opposite end zone, ESPN was set up to do their interview.

I continued with my workout, but it was hard not to pay attention to what was going on at the other end of the field.

Parker tried to keep my focus.

"The cameras aren't for you this time, big guy," Parker told me. "But you better not fall down in front of the crew or Erin Andrews. Wouldn't want them to make you feel embarrassed."

"Ha," I laughed half-heartedly. "I'll be fine walking ten yards," I replied, knowing it would be a challenge to avoid falling, especially being fatigued from the earlier workouts.

"All right, let's do it."

Parker stood at the goal line as I stood up with one cane at the back of the end zone. I took my first two steps fairly quickly. Parker reminded me, "The whole crew just started watching, so don't blow it."

I took my next two steps more cautiously, lifting my right leg and trying to plant my weight on it to avoid the feeling of falling forward. I carefully dragged my left forward next to the right and then raised my line of sight to check my progress. I knew I hadn't made it very far, but I could see beyond Parker that the ESPN film crew was busy setting up, not watching me. I had a sigh of relief and a laugh, with the peace of mind that I could take steps without worrying about who was watching. Mike and Parker continually tried to test me mentally, and I knew this was one of those tests. I had to get used to people watching me if I planned to walk in front of over 110,000 people!

I always enjoyed getting the opportunity to see Elliott practice. I felt special to get to see just how hard these student athletes work to be successful. Here, Parker, Elliott, my mom, and I capture a moment on the practice field.

FALLING FORWARD

Once I reached the goal line, I sat on a stool to catch my breath.

"Get your mind right, we need to do the next ten better than that. Gotta keep those toes pointed forward, and get your left foot in front of your right as much as you can," Parker told me.

Each time my left foot was in front of my right, with the cane in my left hand, I felt the sensation of falling forward and toward my right side. I knew I had to try to do better, and the only way was to face the feeling head-on. I stood up and took two quick steps once again. My feet were lined up next to each other now, but I knew I had to try better with my next two.

Once again, I took a slower right step and then settled in that position as I moved the cane in my left hand a foot in front of my right foot. I tried not to push myself to my right as hard with the cane, hoping I could shift my weight onto my left leg this time. I pulled my left foot forward, my toes just a few inches ahead of my right foot. For a moment, it felt a lot more natural, but the feeling quickly was replaced with the feeling of falling. I felt my body shifting forward, and I immediately tried to press back with my right leg but failed. I rolled into the fall, dramatically letting my legs fly into the air.

"Haha, man, you blew it! But I'm not laughing at you, I'm laughing with you. I'm glad you pushed yourself to get that foot forward anyway! You almost had it that time," Parker said.

He brought the stool over to help me get back up to try again. This time Parker stood to my right as I repeated the process. I tried to fight the feeling once again, but this time I had to reach out to push off Parker's shoulder to keep from falling.

"Stop touching me, man," Parker shouted.

I laughed. "Can't help it, my balance is off today."

The next right step had me feeling as though I would fall back and to the left. Luckily, I was able to quickly recover toward falling forward and into my right step. Before I knew it, I was at the ten-yard line and ready for a rest.

Parker threw a towel over my head after I sat down, then slapped me on the back.

"Nice work, you finally figured that out. Just have to do it a few hundred more times now. At least now you know the muscles work that keep you from falling," Parker encouraged me.

SURREAL SURPRISE

As I was wiping the sweat from my face, I noticed Parker shift his attention behind us, toward the ESPN crew. He was holding his hands behind his back nonchalantly, gestured a head nod, and then asked, "How are you doing today?" toward someone out of my line of sight. I turned my head to see Erin Andrews walking by, smiling at Parker.

"I'm doing great. How are you both doing?" she replied.

Parker said, "I'm doing good. Not sure about this one though. Brock here has been falling down a lot today."

I smiled and looked up. "I'm doing just fine actually," I said, trying not to seem starstruck.

Erin laughed. "Well, that's great to hear. I'm sure you *are* doing great. I read that you are going to lead the team out next Saturday. That is just awesome!"

"Thank you. I'm a big fan, and that means a lot coming from you. I'm blessed to get the chance."

Parker added with a laugh. "We just have to make sure he doesn't blow it and fall in front of all those people. We know he will do fine though, he's been killing it. But now we have to go climb some stairs."

Erin Andrews continued to say how inspiring it was that I took up this challenge. It was great to unexpectedly meet such a famous sports reporter on a day that started out like any other. I still had work to do, and Parker gave me another cane so I could walk over to the stairs. As we were walking, I noticed some players talking to Erin and getting some pictures. Parker smirked at me.

"Do you want to get a picture with her?" he asked.

"No, no ... Too much work to get done. I can get one another time probably. Not sure when, but maybe I'll run into her at some point in the future when I'm not at workouts."

He laughed. "Let's walk over there, and I'll ask if you can get a picture."

As we approached the group in between pictures, Erin actually approached us.

"Could I get a picture with you, Brock?" she asked.

I was stunned.

Parker told her, "We were actually going to ask you the same thing, but Brock here was too shy to ask."

Erin handed Parker her phone as I stood next to her to pose for the picture.

Erin told me, "If you want, I can just send you the picture if you give me your number."

Parker stepped in, "No, that's okay. Got my phone right here. I can take another one for Brock."

"Thanks, Parker," I said sarcastically.

We thanked Erin for the picture and headed back to the stairwell to continue the workout. Parker laughed along the way.

"Sorry for stepping in there. Didn't think about you being able to text Erin to chat sometime. Thought it would be easier that way," he apologized. "But now we need to climb these steps."

After finishing the steps, I finished my workout with some stretching. I also rested my feet on the Power Plate, which helped with circulation and stimulating the nerves in my legs.

Often during this time, I realized how much I just wanted to lie down and sleep because I was so worn out. But at the back of my mind, I knew it was important to keep pushing myself. Having the discipline to finish this work would be beneficial, even though I couldn't know when or how. On that day, it paid off to stay a little longer for my workout. As I was leaving, Erin Andrews was just leaving the building as well.

"Thank you again for the picture, it really is amazing what you have been able to do," she told me.

"Thank you, it is pretty awesome I will be able to share the moment with everyone. I've been given so much opportunity and hope, so I want to share it with everyone else."

"Have you been able to do any motivational speaking to share your story?" she asked.

"I have actually, which I never thought I would do. I've spoken at my high school, churches, and a bunch of other events so far. It's been a great way to have an impact, I'm just amazed by it."

"Well, I know there are so many great speakers in sports—coaches, broadcasters, and players—but they don't have the story you have. You could make a career out of it because your story is so inspirational."

Until then, I hadn't thought seriously about speaking as a career. I mostly spoke here and there, when someone I knew asked me. When I sat in my car, I thought about what could come after my walk in the Big House. I had already made plans to keep working out, but there would have to be something else. Speaking was something very rewarding, and I realized if I could actually make a career out of it, I would love my job.

BACK TO WORK

On Saturday, one week before the opening game, Michigan was having a walk-through for all the pregame festivities. I arrived at the east tunnel that morning, anxious to get this trial out of the way before having a huge crowd watching. I rolled down the tunnel in my wheelchair, surprised at how many people there were—band members, stadium staff, players, coaches, police officers, and students.

Once I was at the end of the tunnel, I was shocked to see how many students and players' family members were in the stands. It wasn't a big enough crowd to even fill the front row around the stadium, but it was enough to make me nervous. I tried to imagine the rest of the seats filled as I sat near the edge of the football field. The thought terrified me. I tried to take my mind off it as they started the game clock and made announcements of when things were set to happen.

One of the stadium employees came up to show me the itinerary for the following week. They would show a short clip at the 8:45 mark. I would come into the stadium from the tunnel with eight minutes remaining, then have three minutes to reach the banner.

The clock was at around twenty minutes, so I went to get in position in the tunnel. Band members were already waiting there, along with some students holding the banner I would be walking to. Some of them came up to say hi and shake my hand as we waited, which helped to calm my nerves. Before I knew it, they were ready for me.

I rolled out toward the edge of the field and placed my feet on the turf. As the announcer made the introduction, I stood and began walking with two canes out to midfield. I seemed to walk faster than I typically would, but I felt great about it. I stood off to the side as they finished announcements and started to think again about how many people would be there the following week.

It was overwhelming.

I was relieved when Parker told me I could rest that week and just come in one day for a warm-up. That way I would be at 100 percent on game day.

BROCK'S RULES FOR STRIVING FOR THE IMPOSSIBLE

1. **Surround yourself with supportive people.** There comes a time when you need to have an accountability partner whom you trust enough to push you beyond those limits. From the first day we started working together, Mike and Parker could only see the end goal. They weren't fazed by any negative outlooks or limitations. Eventually, they pushed me beyond what my brain and body thought was possible. I stopped "hitting walls" because they no longer existed for me either.

- Create a list of people whom you trust enough to push you beyond your limits.
    - Reach out to them and tell them what you're working toward and where you might get stuck.
    - Ask them how you can support them in the same way.
    - Set up some small steps you can each take, and put some dates on your calendar.
    - Don't give up on yourself the same way you won't give up on them.

2. **Decide what failure actually means to you.** When I first started working out with Mike, I told myself that no matter what the outcome, I knew I would be in the best shape I could possibly be, whether I still needed a wheelchair or not. He always had a way of showing me that when something unexpected happened, it was a new learning experience. When I fell off the exercise ball early on, he simply said it was a success because it taught him something about what my body did. Trust me, if you're going to stand up, you're automatically going to risk falling. But what matters most is that you *keep getting back up.*
    - Journal about the lessons you've learned when you've faced setbacks or challenges in your life.
    - If you feel discouraged, take a moment to remind yourself how far you've come.
    - Choose your "hard."
        - What are you willing to push yourself past a wall to achieve?

CHAPTER 8

LEADING THE TEAM

The day of the game was incredible. I arrived in Ann Arbor in the morning and met up with some friends and the ESPN and Big Ten Network camera crews. We were tailgating, and I handed out some of the shirts I made. I hoped the shirts would raise some curiosity and allow my friends to share the story during and after the game. The cameras were drawing attention, and I planned to go on the radio in an hour, around noon. I was glad to have a group of my friends there to experience the day with me. It just wouldn't be as great without having the people with me who had gone through so many ups and downs.

As the cameras followed us to the corner of Stadium Avenue and Main Street, people were watching us and pointing, wondering why the cameras were following us. We all kept telling them not to miss the pregame.

There was a stage set up for me to sit down with the radio personalities. They put me at ease, telling me they would ask some questions and I could answer as if there wasn't a big crowd watching and listening on the radio. As I positioned myself on the stage, I became more relaxed when I noticed my friends waving at me and trying to make me laugh. I was only onstage for a few minutes, but I got to share bits and pieces of my story. I was also able to think about how I felt about everything and, more importantly, to thank all the people who helped me get to where I was.

When I got offstage, there were even more people staring, wanting a picture, or asking about my story. It was amazing to me that so many people were so interested in what I was doing when everyone was there to see Michigan and Connecticut play football in a few hours.

I thought we had plenty of time as we made our way toward the stadium. We stopped every now and then to shake hands or take a picture, but mostly the cameras just filmed my friends and me joking around on the way. Time flew by as we wandered, and I realized I only had about thirty minutes to get to the tunnel.

GETTING TO THE TUNNEL

We were on the south side of the stadium, so it wouldn't be a problem to get there in time. However, I didn't realize that recent construction made going around the southeast corner nearly impossible, as you had to go down a lot of steps or a steep hill to go around. I decided I should try to go in through the stadium itself, but I didn't know whether they would let me. The first lady taking tickets told me I couldn't go in that way without my ticket, and I couldn't exit and return if I had to get out. This was when I started to feel somewhat stressed.

As I discussed what I should do with my friends, one of the attendants in yellow came up and asked what the problem was. I explained how I needed to get to the tunnel and why it would take so long to go around. He stopped me as I was giving the details and said he would personally escort me into the stadium and to the elevator so that I wouldn't have to worry about time. It was a huge relief! He waved at another man he worked with and told him to help clear a path for me to move through.

It was remarkable—I felt like a big deal being escorted through the lines and crowds. We were at the elevator in no time and took it down to the parking level. Once we exited the East Suite Lobby, the tunnel was directly to our right. There was a line to get into the tunnel area, but after giving my name to the man with the list, I was allowed in right away.

I thanked the two men for getting me there so quickly, but they insisted it was their honor to help me and wished me luck.

I had no time to really think about what was about to happen with everything moving so quickly. I finally had time to settle down and think when they told me I could wait in the press green room under the stadium. I sat in my wheelchair and bowed my head to pray.

There was a lump in my throat, butterflies in my stomach, and I was sweating as if I had just had a workout. I was still wearing my long-sleeved "Impossible is Nothing" shirt, hoping it would absorb the sweat. I continued to keep my head down as I prayed for the nerves to go away before I had to walk out.

My mom arrived about fifteen minutes later, followed by my older brother, Blake, and his wife, Molly. I continued to sit in silence, hoping it would help me calm down. I noticed the cameras had arrived, but they remained out in the hall, filming from a distance. Every time I started to feel better, the rumblings of the crowd made me feel uneasy.

I took deep, slow breaths, thinking about all the work that had led to this moment. I thought about all the falls and failures and how I always got back up and continued to fight. I remembered all the times I had someone who believed in me and was there to help lift me back up, as well as how far I had come since the hospital.

I remembered the sleepless nights when I would envision this day—an impossible moment. It was so incredible, so surreal, and so far beyond what I could have imagined in my wildest dreams. I hadn't even felt the full experience yet—it was just the lead-up to the moment.

"Brock? We are ready for you to come out to the tunnel," a lady peeking her head into the room said. "The team should be going out for warm-ups soon, so you may see your brother."

"Thank you," I told her, still staying on the quiet side with my nerves rattled.

I felt somewhat better in the tunnel, especially once the players started to emerge. Each one came out of the locker room from the opposite side of the tunnel instead of making a sharp left and came out of their way to give me a handshake, a hug, or a high-five before going to warm up. It helped take my mind off the stress and made me feel like a part of the team.

REFLECTION AND REVERENCE

I knew what an honor it was to enter the field with the team, but it reminded me how much they had always made me feel welcome. It gave me strength to know that the moment was meant not just for me but for everyone who had been a part of my life.

My family had been through so much. All my friends had been there for me. Even all the people who came to the game would be impacted by seeing this goal come to fruition. It felt like so much pressure being in front of all these people, but I knew overcoming it would be well worth it.

Once most of the team was already on the field, I saw Parker walking out. He looked right at me with a straight face and came right toward me.

"Hey, brother," he said as he bent down to give me a hug. "I love you, man. This is your moment. Proud of you."

Mike followed right behind, giving me a big hug.

"Thank you for everything, Mike," I told him.

"You did it, Brock. You put in the work. You had faith. Here you are. Love you, and couldn't be prouder to have gotten to work with you. How are you feeling? Nervous? Scared?"

"Terrified," I answered. "I keep wondering what happens if I fall or how I'm going to feel as I get out in front of that crowd."

Mike stopped me there, saying, "Let me tell you something. It doesn't matter if you fall, at this point, you *cannot* fail. If God is for you, who could stand against you? *No one!* Every person in that crowd is going to be cheering for you. After that, they're going to be rooting against someone, but *not you*. They'll cheer for you to walk, they'll cheer for you to get up if you fall, and they will continue to cheer no matter what happens. Everyone wants you to succeed and see faith rewarded. You've already succeeded, bub."

I felt a huge shift in the weight on my shoulders at the thought. It was hard to tell if the weight was lifted or if I had simply been given the strength to carry it. Either way, it was empowering, and it renewed my faith to finally accept Mike's view on the situation. I took in the realization that no one wanted to see me fail. Everyone was for me, not against me.

Understanding that I didn't achieve this moment on my own gave me faith and confidence that I was where I was meant to be, giving me the courage to overcome my anxiety and fear.

As I made my way down the tunnel, I began to hear the crowd grow louder, and I could start to see them. Outside the tunnel, I noticed Lisa Salters, who had interviewed our family for *E:60*, standing near the field. She noticed me as well and came over to say hello.

"How have your workouts been going? Such a great day for your big moment," she said.

"It is an amazing day," I replied. "Workouts keep getting tougher, but I have started to improve each month, each week even. Hard to believe the game is already here."

She could sense the uneasiness in my voice, and she knelt down next to me, looking out over the field in front of us.

"You know, I remember how nervous I felt the first night I was asked to do a live courtside broadcast ... "

She went on to tell me that she had been waiting for that moment but still was very nervous. She said Kobe Bryant noticed her nervousness and came over to talk to her. He told her they chose the right person for the job and that she was going to be great. It calmed her nerves before she went on. She realized it was an incredible moment she needed to enjoy and make the most of, and she did. She told me this was one of my great moments and to cherish it.

I thought I already felt good, but her sharing that with me really made me feel great about everything that was happening—especially knowing that she took the time before the game, noticing that I was nervous, to help me enjoy a moment that otherwise might have been harder to enjoy. I let go of even more of the stress I had felt and began to take everything in rather than block out the crowd and festivities.

I made my way back to the tunnel as the clock ticked down.

I was just inside when I saw the band walking down to the entrance to the field. A man with a beard was holding a camera next to me. He leaned over to tell me he couldn't wait to see me walk out there and shook my hand. I was surprised to realize it was Rupert Boneham, a four-time contestant and fan favorite from the television show *Survivor*.

I had to laugh to myself, realizing how many people were excited for my big moment. It was crazy to me how big this dream had grown, and I was just a few minutes away from living it. The band started its cadence, the drums sending chills through my body and getting my adrenaline going.

I heard the announcer in the background introducing the band.

They were marching in place in front of me, then marching out of the tunnel. I found it hard to distinguish between the drums and my heartbeat.

The band came to a halt once lined up outside the tunnel, across the field. It grew eerily quiet outside the stadium, as the clip began to play, showing me doing some workouts. They cued me to come out to the edge of the field, my eyes gazing around the stadium, finally seeing it filled to capacity.

TAKING THE WIN

It was surreal and overwhelming. My mom leaned in from behind me to give me a hug, tears of joy in her eyes. My brother Elliott came up and grabbed my shoulder, as did my older brother, Blake. We smiled at each other and then looked at the big screen. The clip was finished, and the announcer introduced us. The crowd erupted as I began to stand up.

The feeling as I looked toward the banner, nearly sixty yards in front of me, was surreal. Elliott had tried to describe what running out onto the field was like for him, but he told me it was unlike anything he had ever experienced. That's how it was for me too. I tried to maintain composure but felt an adrenaline rush unlike any I had ever felt before.

The sound seemed to fade out as I took my first step. I suddenly had tunnel vision—my peripheral vision was not only blurred, but the color of the banner seemed to be enhanced. Each step seemed to come automatically, one after the other, easier than they ever had.

I looked up at the banner between steps; it felt like I was floating toward it. All the emotions of joy and pain seemed to come to me simultaneously. The thought of our tragedy came back, but I was overcome by the joy of achieving an impossible feat in that instant. I felt tears welling up, adding to my blurry vision, but I could tell the banner was getting closer.

Time seemed to slow down, but I still couldn't take in everything at once. As slow as I was walking, it felt like I was instantly transported to the banner once I was there. I paused underneath it and slowly reached up with my right hand, the strap of the cane around my wrist. I lightly touched the banner, then pulled my hand back to slap it as so many legendary players at Michigan had before me. The immense crowd noise came back, as did my vision and everything around me.

I had finally reached my goal!

The band began to play as I walked to the side of the crowd, seeing the team start to rush toward the banner. I stood on the edge of the field as my wheelchair was brought behind me.

I said I was all right to stand and looked toward the flag for the national anthem. I stood proudly, looking over the crowd that had just witnessed my moment, but even more proud that I was able to *stand* for "The Star Spangled Banner."

After the national anthem, I sat back down in my wheelchair. I began to roll off the field. I looked up, in awe of the number of people I shared my moment with. Coach Rodriguez, Mike, Parker, and a bunch of players all patted me on the back as I went off the field. Others would give me a high five, telling me how great I had done.

I tried to take it all in as the game started, and that's when I began to realize just how improbable this moment was. I was a graduate of Michigan's biggest rival, The Ohio State University. I wasn't even really a football player, having only played one year in high school. Then, most improbable of all, was the one-percent chance I had been given of ever walking again.

Molly joined us on the field to take some photos. It was really incredible to see how big of a crowd witnessed that moment.

After touching the banner, I could tell Mike wasn't surprised at all we had accomplished our task, and I could also see how incredibly proud he was having been on the journey with me.

Aunt Sandy

I was walking down the tunnel, and there was a room off to the side. I looked over, and there was Brock, all by himself sitting in a wheelchair, and he had his head down. I knew what he was thinking, and I said, "Brock, it's going to be all right."

He just kind of shook his head. But it was so moving to see him in that wheelchair and looking out over 110,000 people in that stadium, knowing he had to prove not only to himself but to everyone else that he could walk across that field.

That was a moment for me that I will never forget. He got up, and he did it.

Elliott

The day Brock walked out on the field, I was nervous, obviously, but the whole team had seen how much work he'd put in. Coach Rodriguez had challenged him at spring practice in front of the whole team, "Brock Mealer, we're gonna challenge you to lead the team out."

At the point of that challenge, Brock was walking maybe five yards at a time and had the "Forrest Gump" metal braces around his legs. I remember thinking, *He's gonna lead the team out? Are you out of your mind?*

But then there was Brock, again, not complaining, just saying, "All right, how are we gonna make this happen?" He knew he would have to work out even harder and take more risks.

Watching the progress he'd made up to the day he walked out, I knew even if he had fallen, we were going to just pick him up. It's nothing we hadn't seen before. And we were gonna make sure he finished and touched the banner. No matter what happened, we were going to be proud of him.

In many ways for our family, it was a full-circle moment. It provided another layer of healing, I think because it just felt like all of our hope was in Brock. That moment was kind of a payoff, even though he was the one putting in all the work.

It was kind of a deep breath for us all. It wasn't the end of wanting him to walk and continue to make progress. But it was just a huge healing moment. And it just felt like a victory after everything we'd been through. We fought to get the best possible outcome after a horrible tragedy, and Brock led the way.

Mom

When we walked across the field, Brock didn't know if he could make it because you couldn't talk to him when he was walking. He had to think about every step. If he was thinking about what you were saying, then he might miss one. So with all the noise, he was so worried that he wouldn't be able to do enough thinking in his head to get his legs up there.

I just didn't want him to fall. But the moment we started walking across, all I could feel was Brock's dad, David. I felt like he was walking right beside me. And he was just so proud. It felt like we crossed a finish line. All my pushing, all the people who told me I was crazy—it was all okay then. They all knew the truth. Brock could walk.

GIVING GOD THE GLORY

As I worked back through the challenges I had faced in my life, especially all the days my body felt like giving up, my mind tried to grasp how I had reached this moment and what steps I took to achieve this victory over such an overwhelming number of obstacles along the way.

I started to think about how hard I had worked to get here, how many times I had collapsed and even struggled to just crawl. I thought of all the people who pushed me and gave me opportunities when I needed them most. More than anything else, somehow, I could *feel* my dad and Hollis smiling down on us that day.

I can't explain it, but somehow I knew they weren't surprised at all by the events. And in knowing that, I realized everything leading up to this point wasn't by chance. As much as I grappled with the accident happening and numerous other unanswered questions, this moment had nothing to do with luck, coincidence, or even just hard work. It had *everything* to do with God.

I remembered the verse on the back of my shirt, Mark 9:23: *Everything is possible for one who believes.* My faith had continually brought me back to that verse as I faced an impossible task. When I would feel doubt overwhelming me as I struggled, I tried to come back to the truth given in that verse.

Rather than trying to bargain or asking God to let it happen, I simply believed those words of Jesus and continued to work. Although I wasn't able to run or jump that day, I was still given more than I felt like I deserved. I realized this was the start of something incredible, something beyond me, and I wasn't going to let it be the last goal.

INCREDIBLE SUPPORT

As I took my attention back toward the game, I quickly realized I could only see it on the big screen. I was surrounded—players and staff in front of me, the stadium seating behind. It reminded me to make my way off the field to my seats where some of my friends were waiting.

When I turned, I recognized one of the faces nearby. I wouldn't have thought I would be surprised by anything after what had just happened, but several yards away, I saw Superman! Actor Dean Cain was standing several yards away, just to my left. I grew up watching *The Adventures of Lois and Clark*, so it was easy to recognize him.

"I wonder if we can ask for a picture, or would that be rude during the game?" I asked my brother Blake as I started to head toward that direction.

"Hi, Dean, I didn't want to interrupt the game for you, but I wondered if we could get a picture with you?"

"Of course, not a problem at all," he responded.

"I'm a big fan, and I'm definitely partial to Christopher Reeve for all he's done, but it's crazy to have Superman here for my walk after my own spinal cord injury."

"Oh, I'm partial to him too, but look at you! That was great, *you're Superman!*" he told me as we started to pose for a picture.

I laughed. "I don't know about that, but thanks!"

With Blake, meeting Superman, Dean Cain, on the sideline shortly after my walk out to touch the banner.

I couldn't think of a much better compliment at that moment. What were the actual odds of that happening on the same day? Less than one percent, I bet. It was amazing to think that the man who followed Christopher Reeve in the Superman role just happened to be at Michigan's football game that day. I smiled as we continued to make our way off the field toward our seats.

We had only made it a few feet before we were stopped by a sideline reporter—Heather Cox. I recognized her from TV but forgot I was told they might want a few quick words.

She told me how awesome it was to see me walk out onto the field and asked if she could just ask me a couple of quick questions. Of course, I was happy to do it. I was humbled just to be asked. She explained that they had to wait for a short break between plays, and then she'd ask how it felt to be out there.

I was overwhelmed by everything that happened in that short time, so it was a relief to get back to my seat with all my friends. Along the way, a few people would say hello or tell me what a great job I did. I had the most satisfaction from those who were able to see the shirt and would simply say, "Glory to God!" or "One percent!"

We enjoyed cheering for Michigan (although many of my friends were still Ohio State fans, so I won't speak for them) and were able to watch the team earn a victory. If they were anywhere near as amped up as I was at the start of the game, there could be no doubt they would win.

I felt extremely privileged that I was able to see how hard the team worked in the offseason to earn this victory and to know that they were able to see me put in work during the last year to earn my own victory.

As great as it was to reach that particular goal that day, I began to feel even more excited about what would come next. Touching the banner seemed to be the entrance to the boundless opportunities I had prayed for so often, freeing up my future.

For the longest time, my goal was to walk again—plain and simple. The day I touched the banner was the symbolic moment of overcoming the one-percent chance I had been given and being able to once again stand for the national anthem. It was an incredible day, to say the least. But I always knew there was something bigger at play.

MY NEXT SEASON

Throughout the grueling workouts, the only thing Mike asked of me was that I pay it forward by sharing my gifts with someone else.

I remember thinking, *I have nothing to give. I'm just here struggling to make it through my days, sometimes minute to minute.*

He would remind me that he was there to help me get there, and I would know what it was one day. He wanted to make sure that I didn't hide my gift once I figured it out.

I was about to enter a new phase of my life. And without being able to see the view through the clouds, I kept looking up and started moving in faith toward my next mountain.

CHAPTER 9

OPPORTUNITIES ABOUND

About a year after the accident, and well before my monumental accomplishment of walking onto the UM field, my former high school principal asked me to come and speak to the students for a Thanksgiving assembly. The idea was that my coming in to share what I was thankful for could have a big impact on the kids, given that most—if not all—of them knew of what my family had gone through.

After considering it for a few weeks, I felt a strong pull leading me toward a yes, so I agreed. After letting them know I'd do it, my nerves took over, and my anxiety started to increase. At one point I even considered calling in sick, like I used to try and do when I was a student myself.

But then I thought about the powerful story of gratitude I had to share and what it might mean for the students. Many of them had sent prayers and cards or banners to show their support after the tragedy, and I knew this was a chance to give back to them.

The big day arrived, and I made my way over to the school, where I was met by the principal and some staff members. Their warm and friendly welcome eased my nerves somewhat as we made our way to the old, familiar auditorium, and I watched the students file in. Cue my stomach butterflies again!

After being introduced and coming onstage in my wheelchair, I opened with what I thought was a pretty good joke:

"I just rolled in from Columbus, and *boy, are my arms tired*!"

I was met with complete crickets. Almost.

The students didn't know what to think. The single laugh I heard was from my former government teacher. The rest of the auditorium was completely silent. I wondered if the teachers had cautioned the students to be on their best behavior before coming into the auditorium, making them unsure of whether they even *could* laugh.

Regardless, the flat reaction to my attempt at an opening joke didn't do anything to bolster my confidence at the moment. But knowing I had to keep going, I took a deep breath and continued. For the most part, I stayed on track, telling the students about how I stayed optimistic and motivated on my difficult days and sharing a few stories about my journey to this point.

While recounting the accident, I looked up and noticed some faces in tears, which made me start to choke up a little too. It certainly wasn't my intent to make people cry, but it was understandable that they did. Some of these students were classmates of Eliott and Hollis, including Hollis's two younger sisters, who I assumed were in the audience. I had to pause and take a moment to compose myself.

I had written some talking points on a note card to try to keep me focused, knowing ahead of time that my own emotions might make things more challenging. My mom insisted I have them with me, and I was glad when I saw them in my left hand as I wiped my eyes with my right one. I talked about my workouts at Michigan and being thankful for all the support I received from the team. I talked about the banner and cards I received from so many of them and thanked them, letting them know I had hope for the future.

Before that day, it never crossed my mind that I could leverage my experience after the accident to potentially encourage and inspire others. But when I left the school, a new seed of opportunity had been planted, and there was a part of me that was curious about what it could grow into.

Aunt Sandy

I've listened to Brock several times when he speaks to groups, and I still get emotional every time I hear him. I look at the young people in the audience listening so intently to what he has to say. If he can reach just ten or fifteen people about how important it is to never give up on yourself and have faith, they'll do just fine in life.

He is a wonderful and inspirational speaker. He has inspired our entire family and the whole community. Several years back, I went to hear him speak at Springfield High School, right outside of Toledo. The kids were mesmerized by this six-foot-three guy coming out with crutches. They knew the story because it was in all the papers. As he spoke to them, I just felt like this was his calling. Reaching some of these young people and touching them in a way that will enhance their lives is such an incredible gift.

MORE UNEXPECTED OPPORTUNITIES

After walking onto the field, I began to get back into a more normal routine. It was still refreshing for me to hear support from various people I passed during the day. In my day-to-day life at this point, I continued to be encouraged by friends and even strangers who knew my story. In addition to interacting with these supporters in public, I was overwhelmed with support through social media as well.

About a month after I walked out, a woman contacted me through social media and told me about a fundraiser that was being held at a local sports bar.

A six-year-old boy, Jack, who had been going through chemotherapy was a big Michigan fan, and this woman thought my attendance would mean a lot to him. I wasn't convinced my attendance would really matter all that much, but it was a great cause, so I definitely wanted to be a part of the support. I had no clue how significant the event would be, not just for Jack, but for me as well.

When I arrived at the restaurant, it was already packed with people, which made it difficult as I tried to walk in with two canes. There were silent auctions, games, and a DJ on the loudspeaker between songs—so much excitement in the room! I found an empty table just left of the entrance to sit down and order a meal.

As I was finishing up my meal, the woman who invited me to the event came up to greet me.

"Jack will be so excited you've come! You really have no idea what it means to him."

A short while later, the DJ announced that a special guest was there to support Jack. I looked around to see who they were going to acknowledge, and to my surprise, he announced my name, along with a brief description of my journey. I reluctantly stood up to wave, thinking I wasn't worthy of such notice. It was a great honor just to be invited to share the night with Jack and his family.

As the night went on, I continued to be introduced to several people until I finally got to meet Jack. He thanked me for coming, and I told him how glad I was to be a part of it. It was clear he was worn out from all the excitement of the night. His dad was just about to take him home but stopped to say how great it was to have me there. It really was inspiring to meet a kid with the amount of courage he clearly had, dealing with more than most of us could even imagine at that age.

It was shortly after the fundraiser when Jack's parents sent me an email. They wanted to thank me again for coming that night. They told me that the next day Jack kept talking about how great it was to have me at his event. I was surprised by the impact my visit had.

Jack's parents said that when he went for chemotherapy, they would explain that just like I went to workouts with the Michigan football team to get better, this was Jack's plan for treatment. Hearing this was a humbling and honoring moment for me and made me realize just how much my journey could impact someone else.

There was nothing I could imagine that would be more important than having that kind of influence on someone's life. As I thought about it, I began to consider how much impact my story could have on people if I truly was engaged and believed I was capable of inspiring people on that level.

I never could have imagined having that impact on even one person, let alone many. I realized God had a plan far beyond anything I had imagined. Now more than ever, I began to consider what I would do with that influence.

MOVIE PREMIERE

I continued to work out and get stronger each day. In the meantime, I tried to share my story as often as I could. I was invited to speak to schools, churches, and other organizations each month.

I was amazed at the conversations I had with people who had heard me speak and the way they said they were inspired. It gave me more faith and motivation as well and the courage to continue to get in front of crowds to share my emotional story. I was constantly in awe of the places I was invited, knowing that God had given me an abundance of opportunities.

Another incredible opportunity came my way in September of 2011. I was invited by a friend to come visit Winter the Dolphin at the Clearwater Marine Aquarium for the premiere of *Dolphin Tale*, the movie in which Winter was the star.

If you don't know, Winter was rescued in December 2005, off the coast of Florida, having been caught in a crab trap at only two months old. The trap caused severe damage to her tail, which eventually required amputation. Despite the odds, Winter survived and adapted to a unique prosthetic tail, becoming an inspirational figure and symbol of perseverance and resilience.

It was a once-in-a-lifetime chance to be part of a major movie premiere, so I gratefully accepted. Coincidentally, it was also my birthday.

My friend and I dressed up for the red carpet event, which we knew would be amazing, but we were still in awe of all the people we had the chance to meet. In addition to meeting a number of the stars of the movie, we were able to meet some of the people whom Winter had inspired over the years.

Being able to meet these stars, and realize they are humble, sincere, and genuinely good people, was something I appreciated. Despite not knowing who I was, each one was still glad to speak to me and pose for a picture. The night flew by, and we couldn't thank the CEO of the Clearwater Marine Aquarium enough for inviting us to be a part of this special event.

Visiting Winter the Dolphin at the Clearwater Marine Aquarium.

SOMETHING BIGGER THAN MYSELF

More and more speaking engagements were coming my way. It was always a challenge to tell my story only to have the crowd in tears. I didn't want people to feel sadness, because that made it more difficult to take them to a place of inspiration or motivation.

With more time and experience, I learned how to lift an audience's emotions back up. I emphasized how I was able to gain the strength to overcome and find purpose through the struggles.

To me, this creates a much stronger connection with people and a more powerful, lasting effect. Just as with my injury, I was shown a path that let a weakness or flaw become a strength with time and effort. I started to read the audience, which helped me gauge when I could insert an emotional story or when it was time to bring in my sense of humor or an uplifting story.

After so many events, I felt better about my ability to adjust how I spoke, or even the stories I told, depending on whether the crowd was getting distracted or feeling too emotional by the tragic parts.

Then came the pandemic.

My first event after the devastating effects of COVID was in East Palestine, Ohio, in January of 2021. I was not prepared for the challenge of speaking to a crowd whose faces were covered by masks. It was impossible to gauge their feelings. Deeply focused, sad, happy, or simply indifferent to what I was saying—it all looked the same.

The principal was excited to have me there. He felt like my story could give his students a different kind of hope that had the potential to help them get through different situations that they were dealing with. Because we were under COVID protocols, I didn't have the chance to speak with any of the students after that event.

I often wonder if there was someone in the audience who needed to hear what I had to say that day and if God put me there just for them. Sometimes we don't get to know whether something we did or said had a positive effect on another person. But other times we do.

RIGHT PLACE, RIGHT TIME

Speaking to a group of middle school students continued to be nerve-racking for me. One such event at a local Character Council assembly was the largest student audience I had. The room was packed, and there were even people sitting in the aisles. I always feel anxious when I'm going to speak to kids, even more than adults.

I worried about losing their attention and having an auditorium of kids getting out of control while their teachers looked at me like, *What are you doing? We're giving you the floor, and this is what happens!*

But of course, those fears are just in my mind. A few times when they started getting restless, I was able to regain their attention by talking about meeting Winter the Dolphin, getting to work out with the linebacker for the Pittsburgh Steelers, or about getting to talk on the phone with Coach Tressel.

The theme that day was about having a positive attitude and trying new things. I encouraged them to practice speaking as kids, just to see what it was like. I talked about what it was like for me as an adult when I fell and what it was like to crawl across the floor. I encouraged them to try all kinds of new things. Whether they felt like they were good at something or not, they could commit to getting better. I explained about committing to working with Mike. I wanted them to understand that as kids, the best time to take risks without worrying about other people's thoughts was *now.* It was special to me because there were students who stayed after I was done to have me sign their notebooks.

A year later from that day, I was eating dinner in my hometown. As I finished eating, the waitress came up to me without the check. "There's a young man who wants to pay for your dinner."

I accepted the unexpected gift. He and his mom came to my table, and I thanked him. He was pretty quiet, but his mom was so overcome with emotions she couldn't talk.

She returned to my table a second time after she had composed herself. She told me about her son and his struggle with depression the year before. She tried to do different things to help, but she felt hopeless seeing him so down and not being able to find a solution. He was bullied and struggled with his grades.

She said that the day I spoke the year before, he came home and made a complete turnaround. He asked to join the soccer team. That floored her—he had just told her he didn't want to get involved in sports because he didn't have any friends. She was so thrilled to see the change in his mindset that she didn't question it. He was feeling better, and she just accepted it.

When she went to the parent-teacher conferences a few months later, his mom was happy to hear that his grades were getting better and he was participating more in class. When the teacher asked her if she knew what caused the drastic change, she admitted that she didn't know why but was so glad to hear he was doing better.

The teacher said the Character Council assembly was the catalyst for his changes. When she shared that with me, it made me realize the importance of that day for him. I pushed through my anxiety and spoke that day, probably because God knew what I was about to say would touch his heart. I'd love to cross paths with him again and see where he is now. I've never forgotten that day.

SPEAKING TO THOUSANDS

In the fall of 2015, a friend contacted me about possibly being a part of a political campaign commercial being produced in 2016. Initially, I wasn't very intrigued, but it was for an important office with a candidate I had actually met at Ohio State. He had attended several of our classes while I was a student there, and I felt like I knew him well enough that I said I would be happy to be a part of it. I stayed in contact, but ultimately, it never happened.

In the spring of 2016, the same person contacted me about possibly speaking at the Republican National Convention in Cleveland, as he knew I was a motivational speaker and could fit in well. At this point in my life, I already learned to take every opportunity with confidence. Although I easily could have overthought this particular offer as being far beyond any audience I had spoken to in the past, I told him he could certainly put me down as available.

Over a month later, I was in Florida speaking at a Knights of Columbus event with my friend Tom. The morning of the speaking event, he met me in the lobby where I was having breakfast and dropped a *USA Today* onto the table in front of me. My first thought was that it was a little weird for him to do that because reading the paper wasn't a normal part of my morning routine. But when I glanced at it, I understood his reason: my name was on the headline! The subheading was something to the effect of, "Speakers released for RNC in Cleveland."

My immediate thought was, *What in the world?* I read the article and found a little snippet about my story that they included. Tom joked about the Knights of Columbus getting an RNC speaker at a discounted rate as I marveled at what it would be like to be at that podium. I told him that someone asked me about it, but I didn't know I was supposed to be speaking the next week, let alone on Thursday—the big day of speakers!

After speaking for the Knights, some audience members came up, saying that they heard I was speaking at the RNC. Word sure spreads fast!

Then it hit me. This was happening. And I started questioning why I said I'd do it, wondering what it would entail.

A couple of days later, I received a call from one of the speech writers asking me to send what I planned to say. They told me I had four minutes.

Four minutes? As in, 240 seconds?

I was glad they didn't give me an hour, but four minutes felt like only enough time to say hello and introduce myself. I had to figure out how to navigate that.

In the end, I decided to talk less about my story—which would definitely take more than four minutes—and more about my faith. I wrote very briefly about my story, my faith, and America uniting again as one. I gave shoutouts to The Ohio State University and also to the University of Michigan.

When the organizers informed me that I would be introducing the legendary Bobby Knight via video, I knew I had the opportunity for a little comic gold.

I planned to say, "Man, I'm getting pretty tired. Can someone throw me a chair real quick?" And then, "Oh, there's Bobby Knight!"

The speechwriter didn't get it, so I explained it to her. She didn't want to take a chance on offending him, so it got cut.

I just know Bobby would have appreciated it!

Compared to my other speaking events, this one was on a whole other level. There was so much more activity going on: riding in the SUVs, security personnel and press at every turn, crowds of people everywhere.

On the day of the event, Fran Tarkington, the quarterback for the Minnesota Vikings, spoke right before I did. We were all backstage, looking at a teleprompter and a timer. As each person went onstage and came offstage, the timer adjusted depending on whether they were over or under their allotted time.

Despite all the reasons to feel pressure, I reminded myself that speaking for just a few minutes also was a way to feel less pressure and that I was about 1/10,000 of the actual stage time. I wasn't the main event by any means.

When Fran went out, the timer showed that we were ahead of schedule by seven minutes. But then as he was talking, the teleprompter froze. Twice. So he was ad-libbing until the teleprompter caught up. Twice! I could see he was coming to the end of his speech, so I started to get up and ready for my turn.

Then I saw the clock was at negative two minutes. The people in charge asked me to squeeze my four minutes down. I felt extremely nervous in the moments leading up to it, but much like walking to the banner, I felt amazing walking out to the podium, as though I was made to be there. The lights were blinding, and I felt the sweat on my forehead as I spoke, but the standing and speaking felt seamless.

I had to take a moment, as I was coached prior, just to take it all in. I'm not going to lie—it was very intimidating with the lights, cameras, and too many faces to count looking at me. Yet as I started to speak, everything seemed to happen very naturally, and I didn't feel nervous or tired, until I left the stage entirely and was able to reflect on what I had just experienced.

Luckily, I didn't have any issues with my teleprompter, and I hit my mark. I think the clock might have only been at negative one minute as I walked away from the podium.

With Aunt Sandy at the Republican National Convention in Cleveland in 2016

Aunt Sandy

I've been a political activist for years, and I was a delegate to the Republican Convention, in 2016. I had friends in the Party, and they knew about Brock's accident. So they called me and asked if Brock might be willing to speak at the convention, and I said, "Well, I think he would if he's able to."

So my friend contacted him, and Brock spoke at the National Convention in Cleveland in 2016 in front of 20,000 people in that stadium. He did a wonderful job.

He came down into our delegate section and met all our delegates and shook hands with many of them, including the governor at the time, and Attorney General Mike DeWine, who is our current governor in Ohio

It was a big thrill for him.

LESSON LEARNED

In July of 2018, I was going through a rough patch. My friends decided that instead of sitting at home and moping, I needed to go out to dinner with them. I finally gave in after some prompting from them, and we found ourselves on the patio at a new restaurant in my hometown. After we sat down, I noticed a girl in a wheelchair with her family. I smiled in her direction.

A few minutes later, the girl's grandfather called out, "Hey, Brock!"

When I looked over, the girl and her mom were whispering at him not to bother me with embarrassed looks on their faces as he continued, "My granddaughter works out with your coach."

"Oh, that's cool!" I responded, thinking it must have been one of the physical therapists in town.

After finishing my dinner, I went over to chat with them and found out she was actually working out with Mike Barwis! We got a picture together, and her mom told me more about her story.

The girl, Elle, and her mom lived in Florida. One morning when she was nine years old, she woke up paralyzed due to a virus that was in her spinal fluid. Her doctors said she'd never move her legs or feel them again.

After hearing about what was going on, her grandparents called and told them about me and the work I did with Mike. He just happened to be in Port St. Lucie with the Mets for spring training. When we met in the restaurant, she had been working out with Mike for about a year. She was crawling around on the floor with Mike and had started walking with leg braces, much like I did. It was such a huge deal for her to be able to get where she wanted to go without using the wheelchair all the time.

A few months later, in October, we planned to get together when I went to Florida to walk a mile for a First Steps Foundation Walk and Roll fundraiser. She was using a harness and taking steps with a walker that day and has improved even more since then. It was so cool to see how she was doing and catch up with her main trainer at Port St. Lucie, Bryan Wright, along with Dr. Nick, who walked with me for that mile.

Since then, I've gone down to train with Mike and B. Wright and see Elle. When I was on my way to work out in 2019, I decided to grab a birthday card for her. As we talked during a break, I asked her about school. She told me her favorite subject was science and that she loved learning about the planets. It was such a cool coincidence that I chose a card for her with planets that said, "You're out of this world."

Another time, I told her that I loved animals, and she drew a giraffe for me that I still have today, framed and in my house. It's my mom's favorite animal! We have dinner in that same restaurant we met in every summer. She continues to make great progress, and I always look forward to hearing how things are going with her.

It's awesome to see how being at the right place at the right time happens. And even though we consider them fun coincidences, it's so much more divine intervention. And I'm so grateful to get to experience those moments. Meeting Elle that first day helped me remember that focusing on helping others helps me just as much too.

I met Elle for the first time in 2018, seemingly by coincidence, but I feel that God places special people in our lives right when we need them most.

DIVINE INTERVENTION

Many of my incredible opportunities take the form of speaking invitations. Being asked to inspire an entire school, reinforce a church's faith, or give hope to those who are feeling hopeless has been a great honor for me. It's something I never planned, or even desired at one time. Speaking in front of a crowd was an immense fear growing up, but it was dwarfed by the absolute terror I faced as a result of our tragedy. The experience had given me courage or, more specifically, confidence amid seemingly probable failures, in all aspects of my life.

There never seemed to be a time for me to dream up a pleasant future of any kind, and yet with God's grace, I find myself where I am today. Proverbs 16:9 says, "We can make our plans, but the LORD determines our steps" (NLT).

In my objectively self-seeking plan of wanting to walk again, I can now look back and see how my steps have led me far beyond just the plan of getting back on my feet. My healing has been gradual, and slow, but it has allowed me to share my progress with countless people in that extended period of time.

I don't expect everyone to take my word for it, yet in my own heart, I am sure that luck was suddenly on my side during this time, as I wonder how positive events in my life have come together. There were simply too many specific happenings with perfect timing that had to happen for the results that took place by chance.

When I look back on all the seeming coincidences that have led me to where I am, I begin to see the points where God had given me the signs I had asked for, even though I hadn't noticed them right away.

Over time I've learned to accept acts of kindness from others. A lot of times, people may be cynical about why others want to help them. But instead of thinking, *I don't need your help*, or, *What do you want from me?* I've been able to say thank you and find ways to pay it forward.

Looking back at the opportunities and the incredible people I've met along the way reminds me of the way God puts us in the right place at the right time. Sometimes we get to learn how something we did helped encourage another person. More often we have no idea. But that doesn't mean we shouldn't keep sharing our stories with others.

This poem, often called the Romero Prayer and attributed to Archbishop Oscar Romero, says it perfectly:

> It helps, now and then, to step back and take the long view.
> The Kingdom is not only beyond our efforts; it is even beyond our vision.
> We accomplish in our lifetime only a fraction of the magnificent enterprise that is God's work. Nothing we do is complete, which is another way of saying that the kingdom always lies beyond us. No statement says all that could be said. No prayer fully expresses our faith. No confession brings perfection. No pastoral visit brings wholeness. No program accomplishes the church's mission. No set of goals and objectives includes everything.
> This is what we are about.
> We plant the seeds that one day will grow. We water the seeds already planted, knowing that they hold future promise. We lay foundations that will need further

development. We provide yeast that produces effects far beyond our capabilities.
We cannot do everything and there is a sense of liberation in realizing that.
This enables us to do something and to do it well. It may be incomplete, but it is a beginning, a step along the way, an opportunity for the Lord's grace to enter and do the rest. We may never see the end results, but that is the difference between the master builder and the worker.
We are workers, not master builders; ministers, not messiahs.
We are prophets of a future not our own.[2]

For several years, we hosted a golf fundraiser in memory of my dad to support victims of spinal cord injuries.

BROCK'S RULES FOR STAYING OPEN TO OPPORTUNITIES

I knew that walking onto the University of Michigan football field was just the beginning for me. It reminds me of the movie *City Slickers* when Curly (Jack Palance) tells Mitch (Billy Crystal) that everyone has their "one thing." But it's up to each person to figure it out on our own. Mike Barwis had told me that my "one thing" would just show up as an unexpected opportunity, and I'd know. He was right. So rather than giving you steps to figure out your "one thing," this is my best advice to you:

1. **Keep an open mind.** That first time I spoke at my high school, I was still taking classes at Ohio State and using my wheelchair. I said yes to my first speaking engagement without much hesitation, even though I felt like I might want to "call in sick" instead of putting myself out there.

2. **Accept invitations for new opportunities.** I've said yes to opportunities and then wondered why I'd do such a thing to my future self, but I don't regret one of those quick yes responses when I look back on the experience and the incredible things I would have missed out on by saying no.

3. **Listen to your body.** I've had people DM me asking if I'd like to make millions of dollars by investing in crypto. And I immediately feel a big *nope.* But the day Tom

slapped the newspaper down in front of me, he could see my face light up. Of course, I was nervous, but I was more excited about the opportunity than anything. Listen to yourself if something feels like an absolute no. But if the idea presented to you makes you feel a healthy mix of giddiness and nervousness, go for it! Those little sparks of *Oh yeah! I'm in!* are validation that you are on the right track.

4. **Lean into what you feel passionate about.** For me, it's speaking to people. I have learned a lot since that first day at my high school. But if I decided I wasn't ready back then, I would have missed out on so many incredible opportunities that came after that day when I stepped out of my comfort zone.

CHAPTER 10

COMMIT TO YOUR NEXT MOUNTAIN

When I look back at my life, I can remember many of the challenges and opportunities that made me the man I am today. I always try to stay grateful for the blessings I've had along the way, as well as never forgetting the struggles I was able to endure.

Both of my parents were encouraging and adamant about each of us doing our best in whatever we did. Their belief in our potential extended from grades to sports, and we often heard about how good my mom was at volleyball or how my dad picked up the nickname "Spider" from being a great basketball player.

They both believed we could achieve more, but we would have to be pushed to get there. I realize the reason for them sharing their wisdom, experience, guidance, and discipline was to help us avoid mistakes and missteps.

Our dad was very honest about this truth: the hard work we put into things would determine how good we would become. He was always willing to help and teach but told us we had to be willing to devote the time, practice, and hard work behind our goals.

I never missed a high school basketball practice. I was the first guy there and the last one to leave. I pushed through with taped-up sprained ankles and illness to be the most reliable guy on the team. When I spoke to the team several years ago, it was cool to hear my former junior varsity coach tell the team he remembered that I never missed a practice.

In the summer before my junior year of high school, I decided to try playing football. I had always enjoyed watching but knew little more about it than the average person. I was told how difficult "two-a-day" practices were, as well as how great it was to play under the lights on Friday night. The thrill of the challenge and being with a bunch of my close friends convinced me it would be worth a shot.

Our first week of practicing in full gear was enough to convince me that football might not be my thing. We were practicing form tackling after some warm-up drills, and I loved being able to learn how to tackle correctly. What I hadn't learned soon enough, however, was how to *be* tackled.

After one particular tackle, I suddenly realized I was still attached to the tackler as he began to turn. Josh, who had just pulled away, stopped when he still saw my thumb sticking down through the top of his face mask. Luckily, the rest of me was still attached to that thumb. He took off his helmet, and we walked over to one of the coaches to figure out how to get my thumb out. It was certainly an awkward moment that I would need to avoid in the future. They found it quite humorous—perhaps even borderline talented—that I could somehow fit my thumb into the small gap between the face mask and helmet.

That was it for me.

Or so I thought.

I went home and started to tell my dad, "I don't know how to form tackle. I don't know what it means to pull. I don't know what any of that stuff means. It's miserable." I didn't have time to mention how smelly and nasty the pads were before he responded.

"What are you getting at? You committed to the team. You finish the season, and if you don't want to play next year, that's up to you. But this is the process."

And that was that. I finished the season and didn't go out for football my senior year.

There wasn't one particular incident when I heard my dad's voice in my head as I was working out with Mike, but rather having his words ingrained in my mind over the years made me feel like he was with me, reminding me of the commitment I made when days at the gym felt unbearable.

Honestly, if Mike had shown me the entire program, one workout at a time, from start to finish, I never would have agreed to it. Getting an entire plan would have overwhelmed me. It makes me think of someone working in an office and having their boss walk in with a stack of thousands of sheets of paper that they need to work on, and the employee getting up and quitting.

Luckily for me, Mike only told me about the next thing I needed to do. It was like his stack of papers was hidden in his office and he'd show me one page at a time, or some days just a paragraph, or even one sentence at a time.

I remember asking Mike before we started working out together what I needed to do. His response was, "All you need to do is commit to me 100 percent, and I'll commit to you."

It was okay that I didn't know every little detail because I already learned exactly what it meant to fully commit to something.

Mike said, "Don't put your faith in me. The reason we're doing this whole workout ritual is just a testament to God. We're telling Him we're faithful, we believe this, and we're going to do this."

And we did. I wholeheartedly let go of trying to control things or think about what I could and couldn't do. Instead, I surrendered to each new day, putting my life in God's (and Mike's) hands. I tried to be the clay that would get molded into whatever my life would be. Instead of sitting there asking for healing, we made a pact to put in the work and then let God take me to the next level.

When things got hard, I had Dad's voice in my head reminding me: *You agreed to this. We do not back down.* Other times I couldn't think about anything, but I just kept going.

TAKE YOUR NEXT FIRST STEP WITH GRACE

In the years following the accident, I tried to continue to be the person I always had been—positive, hardworking, and even a jokester at times. But I felt like I failed time and time again. As positive as I would try to be, I would notice myself slipping into depression and feeling bitter about the different circumstances I was dealing with. The inner conflict made me irritable, kept me awake at night, and sometimes left me feeling helpless.

Eventually, I would bounce back. But it didn't change until I finally decided I didn't want to let the accident, my injury, or any of my choices turn me into someone I didn't want to be. That doesn't mean that I only ever have perfect days filled with rainbows and sunshine.

I worked for about a year and a half with a therapist who helped me understand that PTSD wasn't just something that people in the armed forces faced. The *T* standing for *traumatic* could be any kind of trauma that the brain has to process. The accident, the losses we faced, and my injury were all traumatic events. It was great to have someone to talk to and help me understand that I wasn't crazy. It helped me immensely working with my therapist.

If you feel yourself struggling with your mental health, I would highly recommend that you give therapy a try. There are still some issues that stem from my injury itself along with those lingering psychological aspects that can pull me down. I've learned over time to take note of those kinds of negative feelings and thoughts and not put myself down for having them show up.

It's important to remember that any journey you embark on will have its ups and downs. Striving for progress toward your next goal doesn't mean you have to perfectly execute each step along the way. Giving yourself grace during the challenging times is crucial.

It's normal to have moments when you feel like you're falling short or struggling with those inner conflicts when you can see a gap between where you are and where you want to be. It's okay to acknowledge when things are hard and permit yourself to feel those emotions without judging yourself too harshly. Each step forward, no matter how small, is a testament to your commitment and your faith in what is just ahead of you.

WITH A GRATEFUL HEART

It's overwhelming to reflect on the number of people who were able to assist me along the way. Every prayer, even from strangers, gave me strength, courage, and hope. It is hard to explain the hopeless moments I was able to make it through, the nights of anguish and pain from which there seemed to be no escape. But in retrospect, the ability to persevere assuredly came from above.

My need in those moments far exceeded what I was capable of, and the explanation is beyond what we can see but is rather something we can only feel and experience.

Those types of intangible resources cannot be replaced with medicine, technology, or anything else and are priceless.

They can never be repaid, but they can be shared once accepted. That was something I never truly understood until it was shown in such a powerful way, at the darkest moments of my life.

I know that there will be someone, somewhere who will begin to think about the big questions in their own life from reading these words or hearing this story. My sincerest hope is that you will not simply take my word as fact, but instead will seek the truth in your own life.

In finding strength through faith in God through my struggle, I am certain you will be able to do the same. If God was able to show me grace in favor, then He will for anyone willing to seek Him. My journey has grown into something much bigger than I had ever anticipated, which is why I choose to give glory to God, as reflected on the "1%" shirt I wore for my walk onto the Michigan football field. Every person knows in their heart there is a greater purpose beyond the here and now. I encourage you to seek that purpose every day and discover what your mission is.

I will continue to share my story of hope, perseverance, and faith as long as it may bring the comfort and inspiration I have been given. I often feel undeserving of the honor and support I constantly experience, but it always reinvigorates my awareness of the gratefulness and grace I have felt.

I hope that I will be able to spread these supernatural gifts as I share the events in my life that were powerfully and positively affected through faith. Despite ample opportunities to give up and excuses to avoid the mountains placed in my way, I am eternally grateful that I never gave in to either.

I pressed on, with the hope and faith I placed in Jesus Christ, believing there was going to be more to my life than the bleak future I saw ahead. If I had given up at any single one of those moments, I would have missed out on the incredible and abundant opportunities I presently have. No matter how hopeless life may feel, with God, there will always be hope. Even if it's only one percent, there is always hope.

BROCK'S RULES FOR STAYING COMMITTED

1. **Believe in the process.** When you can clearly express why you are determined to reach your next mountain peak, it's easy to remind yourself of those reasons when the climb gets difficult. I knew something good would come out of agreeing to work out with Mike. I didn't promise myself that I would walk. But I did promise myself that I would never regret taking advantage of the opportunity to try and end up where God wanted me to be.

2. **Stay flexible.** I'm guilty of creating rigid plans, especially with my diet. And then when I break a rule, everything just goes out the window. There is a way to bend and then bounce back if you get off track. Life is unpredictable. Instead of looking at setbacks as failures, consider them new opportunities to problem-solve. Some lessons I've learned have been more costly than others, but each one has helped me grow in some way. Make changes and adaptations when the unexpected occurs, and keep moving forward.

3. **Take yourself out of the equation.** Trust me, if I was supposed to go work out on a day when no one else was waiting for me at the gym, I would have stayed home. But that never happened. On the days when it was hard, I considered the people who were counting on me to show up. Think in terms of the impact you can have on someone else's life by staying committed, and you'll understand that doing the thing outweighs your not feeling like it every single time.

4. **Practice positivity.** I remember days when I felt like I was failing, and Mike would turn my perceived failure into a learning experience. When you're working on something important to you, there will inevitably be good days and bad days. Instead of dwelling on what you see as negative or a failure, take a moment to look back at where you started and how far you've already come. Remind yourself that tomorrow is a new day and you can always begin again, with your next first step.

5. **Share your goal out loud.** Choose someone you trust to share your thoughts. Tell them what you want to do and why. Ask them to keep checking on your progress. Knowing that this person will check in on what you're doing from time to time can help you stay motivated.

God's Hands Were All Over This

We can make our plans, but the Lord determines our steps.
—Proverbs 16:9 (NLT)

- Elliott knew God wanted him at the University of Michigan after visiting as a high school junior, and he spoke openly about it.
- Our mom remembers us hugging Dad every time we walked past him, and it crossed her mind that maybe we had to grab all the hugs we possibly could.
- July 4, 2007: Elliott suggested having a Fourth of July party at our house. Mom went all out to make it special, complete with tiki torches. She remembers Dad asking, "Why does it have to be this special?" Her response was, "Well, maybe it'll be someone's last Fourth of July."
- December 1, 2007: West Virginia loses to Pitt. Coach Rodriguez gets an offer to coach at the University of Michigan and asks Mike Barwis to go with him.
- Dad talked to Elliott about honoring his commitment to play Wolverines football after news of the current head coach's retirement came out.

- ➔ December 24, 2007: I went out for a morning run in the snow.
  - Hollis opened her gift from Elliott early at his request.
  - She kept telling our dad to turn on the light in the car so she could admire her new rings on our way to the Christmas Eve party.
  - We lost her and my dad when the old man hit our car.
- ➔ January 2, 2008: Mike is with his West Virginia team for the Fiesta Bowl victory over Oklahoma, then makes his way to Michigan.
- ➔ February 2008: Elliott has shoulder surgery.
- ➔ Early 2008: Mike met Elliott with his shoulder still in a sling and came with him to meet me.
- ➔ September 4, 2010: I led the team onto the field with Blake and Elliott beside me.
  - Mike knew he found his purpose when my hand touched the banner.
  - The Wolverines won 30-10 against the Huskies.

ACKNOWLEDGMENTS

It seems only fitting to conclude this book by striving for another impossible task—thanking all the people who helped make my hope become a reality. I would never be able to include every single person who has contributed to my success, but I want to take the time to thank a few of the many with this opportunity.

First and foremost, I want to thank those who were there for me when my life took a tragic turn. The first responders, some of whom I have had the honor of meeting after the accident, were there Christmas Eve to rescue me from the accident and transport me to the Fulton County Health Center for my initial treatment. Without having men and women willing to respond to traumatic events at a moment's notice, even on Christmas Eve, I would never even have had a chance for my story to continue. Likewise, I wouldn't be where I am today without the hard work of countless doctors, therapists, and nurses who step in to help people in dire situations each and every day voluntarily, yet keep a positive attitude and give their best although their work is never done. To name just a few of those special people: Jacquie, Christy, Sarah, Karen,

Kristina, Ivan, Mike, Jamie, Julianne, Jeff, Rob, Michelle, and Sandy; Dr. Rodriguez, Dr. Abawi, Dr. Abercrombie, Dr. Narayanan, and Dr. Chiodo; and the rest of the team who contributed to my recovery efforts.

It would include an even longer list to share all the visitors I had while in the hospital, let alone those who prayed for me, yet I wanted to also thank a few of them here as well. At the top of my mind, I wanted to thank my close friends: Tyler, Andy, Sarah, Reid, Josh, Brett, Matt, Karen, Jack, Bujar, Jeff, Keith, Eddie, John, Michael, Quinn, Clay, Katie, Sara, Emma, Brittany, Perry, Roger, Jill, Bill, Paul, Mike, Doug, Tom, Rex, Jordan, Justin, Jesse, Linsi, Ami, Deeds, Larry, Patrick, Nick, Denard, Stephen, Tim, and so many more. I was blessed with so much support from former teammates, coaches, officials, and competitors from my time in athletics—and even more from local communities in Ohio and Michigan alike.

There are countless churches, schools, community organizations, and companies that I would like to thank for giving me a chance to share my story with them. I, as much as anyone, realize the value of every moment in time, and they have given of their time and resources to help me realize what a difference this story can make in people's lives.

I'd like to take a moment to thank my family as well—especially my mom, who was a solid foundation through the most tragic season of our lives, and also my brothers, who were with me every step of the way. Both sets of my grandparents—George and Jeanie, Tom and Judy—who taught me so much about life, much of my work ethic, but more importantly, how to be a good person. Their spirit shines through each of us in how we live every day!

Lastly, I want to acknowledge all the people who have inspired me to not only press on toward my goal of walking but beyond that have given me the courage to show up to speak, be filmed by numerous outlets, as well as write this book. From the fellow patients I met while on 6A at the University of Michigan Hospital going through incredible difficulties, to the people I've met through the First Step Foundation that Mike Barwis founded to continue our mission to improve the lives of those that are met with physical difficulties. Time and time again, I feel that God was able to work through people, and oftentimes He would show strength through those who were at their weakest. It has shown me that there are few rewards in life greater than to be gifted with the opportunity to see the positive impact we can make on others.

The "First Steppers," as we proudly call them, have shown me that I'm not alone in facing insurmountable odds. There are others willing to climb the mountain if given the opportunity! From the dozens who came to Schembechler Hall to work out with the Michigan football team—"Doc," Andrew, and Lindsay—to the hundreds of others who followed in our steps from Michigan to Florida to Colorado and beyond.

I've been blessed to connect with so many incredible pro athletes as well, from all levels and sports. It was such a privilege to work out alongside some of the best in the world, watching baseball, football, and hockey players come and go throughout the day. Each of them had their own way of motivating me as I pushed toward my own "trophy" but saw the focus and purpose

I put into each and every workout. There were plenty of athletes who would encourage me in their own way by pushing me to reach my limits, but also by simply cheering me on as they observed my progress from day to day, week to week.

I hope the inspiration I've felt through so many incredible people shines through the words in this book and that the readers will think of the people in their own life that make it so special. Thinking of the people to acknowledge in this section has me wondering where I would be without them, and I'm so grateful God placed them in my life so I wouldn't have had to find out! My journey began so I wouldn't have to wonder, "What if I took that opportunity to do something 'impossible'?" People have often asked if it was worth it, all the sacrifice—the hours and days in the gym, the intense workouts, the sweat and pain of it all. There were some days I wondered about it myself, yet there isn't a doubt in my mind that it was more than worth it, when I see the people we have been able to help.

To be able to give hope to people whom I often see as reflections of my past self has given me more purpose than I could have ever imagined. I feel incredible joy to see someone reach a milestone—standing up for the first time after an injury, drinking a bottle of water on their own, or simply being able to give someone a hug again. My ultimate hope for people I meet isn't necessarily that they will reach 100 percent physical recovery but that we will be able to have them discover that they are 100 percent who they choose to be.

People I meet, whether physically or emotionally injured, often want the same thing I wanted. I thought regaining my ability to walk would make me feel whole, but instead, I found that once I felt wholly myself again, walking slowly came to me as I pressed forward.

As Mike often said, in workouts as in life, "We're seeking progress, not perfection!"

I still face many challenges and struggles in life, but I have always been carried by faith. I truly hope that others will find that faith and purpose meant for their life as well. It seems to me that such a gift is given, not earned, but all are deserving if they simply seek it out. So I encourage you to take that next step. Do not worry about success or failure, but rather, give your all to strive toward your own "impossible" and beyond.

While both of my brothers live in new places, we are still very close; here we are vacationing in Costa Rica in 2022.

I love every moment I get to spend time with family, especially when it is with my nephew, Everett, and niece, Leighton! (L to R: Everett, Grandma Judy, me, Elliott, Mom, Blake, Molly, and Leighton).

ABOUT THE AUTHOR

In 2007, tragedy struck when a car accident on Christmas Eve claimed the lives of Brock Mealer's father and his brother's girlfriend, leaving him paralyzed from the waist down. With just one-percent chance of regaining movement in his legs, the road ahead seemed insurmountable. However, fueled by unwavering faith and supported by the love of his family, Brock embarked on a grueling journey of physical and emotional rehabilitation.

Against all odds, he persevered, defying medical expectations and crafting an incredible comeback story. Two years of intensive therapy led Brock to a pivotal moment in 2010 when he fulfilled his dream of leading the Michigan Wolverines onto the field for their home opener.

Brock earned his undergraduate degree from The Ohio State University in 2008 and completed his MBA at the University of Michigan in 2021. Today he is deeply committed to helping others navigate life's challenges. Through managing his family businesses in Ohio and serving as a board member for organizations like the First Step Foundation, Brock strives to inspire and support those facing adversity. With each step he takes, aided by two canes, Brock is a testament to the power of faith, resilience, and the human spirit.

www.brockmealer.com
Facebook: facebook.com/jointhe1percent
Instagram: Brock.Mealer

ENDNOTES

1 Lewis B. Smedes Quotes. BrainyQuote.com, BrainyMedia Inc., accessed April 30, 2024, https://www.brainyquote.com/quotes/lewis_b_smedes_135524

2 Untener, Ken. "The Romero Prayer." The Archbishop Romero Trust, March 10, 2016. http://www.romerotrust.org.uk/romero-prayer.

Made in United States
North Haven, CT
24 August 2024